E DU

Fairfield 01-02 BHS 306.89

BLAIRSVILLE SENIOR HIGH SCHOOL
BLAIRSVILLE, PENNA

Straight Talk
About Divorce

Other Titles for Teenagers by the Author:

Straight Talk About Cults

*Straight Talk About Post-Traumatic Stress Disorder:
Coping with the Aftermath of Trauma*

Coping with Codependency

Coping with an Alcoholic Parent

Straight Talk About Divorce

Kay Marie Porterfield

☑® Facts On File, Inc.

Straight Talk About Divorce

Copyright © 1999 by Kay Marie Porterfield

All rights reserved. No part of this book may be reproduced or utilized in any form or by any means, electronic or mechanical, including photocopying, recording, or by any information storage or retrieval systems, without permission in writing from the publisher. For information contact:

Facts On File, Inc.
11 Penn Plaza
New York NY 10001

Library of Congress Cataloging-in-Publication Data
Porterfield, Kay Marie.
    Straight talk about divorce / Kay Marie Porterfield.
    p.   cm.
    Includes bibliographical references and index.
    Summary: Discusses the legal, financial, and emotional aspects of the divorce process, examining the impact of divorce on the lives of young people and providing resources for more information and for help.
    ISBN 0-8160-3725-6
    1. Divorce—United States—Juvenile literature.   2. Children of divorced parents—United States—Juvenile literature.
    [1.Divorce.]   I. Title
    HQ834P67   1999   98-45473
    306.89'0973—dc21

Facts On File books are available at special discounts when purchased in bulk quantities for businesses, associations, institutions, or sales promotions. Please call our Special Sales Department in New York at (212) 967-8800 or (800) 322-8755.

You can find Facts On File on the World Wide Web at
http://www.factsonfile.com

Text design by Cathy Rincon
Cover photo and design by Smart Graphics

Printed in the United States of America

MP FOF 10 9 8 7 6 5 4 3 2 1

This book is printed on acid-free paper.

Contents

The advice and suggestions given in this book are not meant to replace professional medical or psychiatric care. Readers should seek professional help if they are experiencing severe emotional or behavioral problems. The author and publisher disclaim liability for any loss or risk, personal or otherwise, resulting, directly or indirectly, from the use, application, or interpretation of the contents of this book.

Introduction

Since 1960 the divorce rate in the United States has tripled. In 1995 alone, nearly 1.2 million couples in the United States ended their marriages. According to United States Census figures, each year more than a million children and teenagers experience the breakup of their nuclear families—families made up of children and the mother and father who conceived them.

Even though this trend may slow, it is expected to continue. Experts who study marriage and divorce predict that nearly half of all marriages in the United States will end in divorce. Currently 40 percent of Canadian marriages end in divorce. Even though divorce rates in the United States and Canada are high, they are higher in Sweden, Finland, Norway, and France. The divorce rate in Russia falls between those of the United States and Canada.

The changes that divorce brings into a young person's life can be difficult and upsetting. Watching parents argue and pull away from one another is stressful. Learning to live in a single-parent home isn't always easy. Neither is adjusting to life in a stepfamily when one or both parents remarry, as they often do.

Just when teenagers need emotional support, patience, and reassurance the most, many of them feel as if no one cares about or understands what they are going through. Some aren't comfortable talking their troubles over with one or both parents because they've never had that kind of a relationship with them. Other adolescents, who are used to sharing their feelings with their parents, find that now Mom and Dad have their minds on other matters, such as hiring a lawyer, negotiating a property settlement, or dealing with the hurt of a broken heart. Parents may be so busy struggling with each other and their own negative feelings during the difficult transition that they don't have a great deal of emotional energy to help their children navigate the stormy waters of the divorce.

Parents don't plan to ignore their children during a divorce, and their lack of attention doesn't signal a lack of love. Some reasons why parents have a difficult time meeting their teenagers' emotional needs when a marriage is coming apart are

- even though they are aware that their children are upset, they don't know how to communicate with them about what is taking place because it is so personal;
- they may be having such a tough time getting in touch with their own feelings about what is happening in their lives and what the future will hold that they aren't ready to talk about it;
- since teenagers are well on the way to adulthood and will be leaving home soon to begin lives of their own, sometimes parents believe the divorce will have little impact on them;
- some mothers and fathers are sure that time, all by itself, will ease the emotional pain a young person feels at watching his or her parents disentangle their lives together and go in separate directions.

In truth, their parents' divorce is challenging to children of any age. The very youngest children may not be able to talk about the stress they feel from that very big change, but they have other ways of showing they're having difficulty, such as nightmares, bed-wetting, and tantrums. Even grown children who moved away from their parents' home years before, and are busy working and raising families, feel some kind of emotional impact on their own lives when their parents' marriage is dissolved.

Young adults face a special set of issues.

- The stress of divorce adds to the turmoil that is simply part of being a teenager.
- Because young adults are mature enough to understand what is going on around them and are better at controlling their impulses than young children, they may appear to be doing fine when they're really not. Facing the facts isn't the same as accepting them, something that must happen before emotional healing can begin.
- Even though a teenager may be falling apart on the inside, if he or she *appears* to have it all together, parents may lean on a teenager for advice and a shoulder to cry on. Hearing the spiteful remarks hurts, but some adolescents are expected to serve as a sounding board for a parent's anger at an ex-, or soon to be ex-, spouse.

Teenagers whose families have recently come apart aren't the only ones who have a difficult time coping. Researcher Judith Wallerstein, who conducted a long-term study of children of divorce, discovered that even though parents may have divorced years ago, emotional ghosts sometimes rise to haunt their children during adolescence, when they begin to be interested in forming romantic relationships of their own. In order to be able to participate in positive and healthy adult relationships, they need to face and resolve the divorce issues they didn't deal with when they were younger.

Although some teenagers may weather the storm of their parents' divorce on their own and suffer no negative impacts later in life, they are the exception rather than the rule. Most people going through times of dramatic change—even adults—need to hear from close friends or a professional counselor that their feelings of confusion, fear, anger, and sadness are perfectly normal. They need to get reassurance from someone they trust that they are not bad or weak for feeling them. The constructive suggestions, feedback, and emotional support that only an objective outsider can give make getting through the hard times and moving on with life an easier process.

Even though the world is filled with knowledgeable and friendly people, help isn't always an easy thing to ask for. Divorce is common today, but it still isn't an easy topic to discuss, especially if you feel as though you're trapped in a war zone. A broken relationship can temporarily trigger angry outbursts and tears from the most level-headed adults. Some teenagers are ashamed of the way their parents behave during a divorce. Young adults who mistakenly think that what their parents do reflects on them sometimes choose to suffer in silence.

Despite the high divorce rate and the fact that many children are raised in single-parent homes today, the stigma of living in a "broken home" persists. Everything from substance abuse to gang violence is routinely blamed on single-parent families. Some adolescents are ashamed that the divorce is taking place at all and worry that their lives will be filled with suffering because their parents couldn't get along.

For teenagers who attend conservative churches or who come from families that believe that "nice" people never get divorced no matter what, the sense of shame they feel when their parents file papers to dissolve their union can be overwhelming enough to make them want to hide. They think that if they keep quiet and pretend the divorce isn't happening, no one will notice or criticize what's happening to their family.

Young people who are determined to be independent often feel they should be able to handle the emotional fallout they are inheriting from their parents' divorce on their own. They believe that to ask for help is a sign of weakness or immaturity, so they have a tough time admitting to anyone, even themselves, exactly how overwhelmed, alone, and helpless they're feeling.

Straight Talk About Divorce was written to provide information about the legal divorce process, the emotions surrounding divorce, and the challenges of living in a single-parent home. Once teenagers have a clear idea of what their family and they are going through, they can make sense of what's happening, know what to expect, and find ways, not only to make the best of the changes, but to use coping strategies that are helpful in other areas of life.

The good news about the major life transition called divorce is that the adjustment process doesn't last forever, and even though life changes after a divorce for teenagers and their families, it goes on.

Young people whose parents divorce find themselves faced with a set of challenges through no fault of their own, but once those difficulties are faced and worked through, life can do more than go on, it can get better with each passing day.

1

Facing the Facts
About Divorce

S elena* thought her parents got along better than most
of her friends' parents. Her mom had gone back to
school and was finishing her teaching degree, and her dad
went trout fishing every chance he got, so they didn't have
a lot of time together. Maybe they didn't talk to each other
very much, but they never argued—at least not in front of
her. They'd been married for 15 years and in Selena's
mind, they were old, so she hardly expected them to hold
hands and gaze into each other's eyes.

She never imagined they would split up—not until the
day she came home from school to find her mom sitting in
the middle of the living room floor crying. She wouldn't
say what was wrong at first, but finally she calmed down
enough to talk.

---

*Everyone identified by first name only in this book is a composite—a por-
trait drawn from details that come from many different people.

"Your dad left us," she said. "He called me from work and told me to pack his things. He wants to be with another woman. She's younger." Then the tears started all over again. "Remember all those fishing trips? He wasn't fishing!"

The next few days were the most difficult Selena ever lived through. Her dad didn't call, and as she watched her mom pack her father's belongings in cardboard boxes and stack them in the garage, crying the whole time, she thought of how she had felt when her grandfather died. That part scared Selena because she was used to seeing her mom calm and in charge.

Even though she felt sorry for her now, she wondered what terrible things her mother must have done or said to him to push her father into the arms of another woman. Hearing all the bad things her mother said about her dad made her sick to her stomach. Even though he was living with a new woman, she still loved him. He was still her father.

She missed him and wondered how he was and what he was doing. If he didn't love her mother anymore, did that mean he'd stopped loving her too?

Jeremy's parents argued over money and politics and who would do the housework. They fought about how to discipline Jeremy and his sister and which grandparents to spend holidays with. They disagreed over what to eat for dinner and what kind of a car to buy.

Most of the time they pulled Jeremy and his older sister right into the middle of their battles, trying to get them to take sides. When they weren't speaking to each other, they used their children to carry messages back and forth.

Sometimes he wondered how they'd ever managed to get together, let alone have two children, they seemed to dislike each other so much. Often he'd secretly wish that they would go their separate ways. Maybe then the house would be peaceful and he wouldn't have to wake up in the middle of the night to loud voices and the sound of dishes smashing against the wall.

They always said that they were staying together for his sake and his sister's. That made him feel guilty that their lives were so miserable. He wasn't sure that he believed in reincarnation, but sometimes he wondered if he'd done something awful in a former life.

At first he was relieved and even excited when his mom and dad announced they were getting divorced, so it didn't make any sense to him when he started jumping at little noises and staying awake half the night. Sometimes he felt angry, and other times he was filled with sadness that he tried his best to hide.

He knew that his parents' divorce was the best thing for everyone in the family, so why was he upset? None of it made sense to him. Maybe he was losing his mind.

Her parents thought she didn't suspect anything, but Bobbi knew something was up when she saw the stack of self-help books on divorce on her mom's nightstand the time she borrowed some hand lotion. Within two weeks, her parents called a family meeting to tell her and her two brothers that they were getting a divorce. They'd worked everything out, they said. All the decisions that needed to be made had been made.

Even though they had problems living with each other and both wanted out of the marriage, they still regarded each other as friends and promised to do everything in their power to ensure that their children would have two parents, they said. Because they wanted what was best for everyone, they would put their differences aside, so that both could continue to raise Bobbi and her brothers.

The children would live with one parent half the year and the remaining six months with the other one. So that the children wouldn't have to change schools, Bobbi's dad had already rented an apartment near the home where they were now living, and where Bobbi's mom would remain. They had even picked a therapist to ease all of the family members through the transition.

The whole business made Bobbi so furious she wanted to hit somebody. If they got along as well as it seemed, she couldn't understand why they would want to be divorced in the first place. The way they talked about it, deciding to divorce sounded less emotional than deciding what flavor of ice cream to buy.

Instead of seeming like real people when they talked, her parents sounded like a pair of psychologists on a television talk show, she thought. They were just a couple of big phonies, and she wished they would get real.

Even though the joint custody idea sounded good at the beginning, she didn't want to give up her room half of the year. She could just imagine herself and her two brothers crammed into an apartment with her dad. Maybe Joe and Robert wouldn't mind because they were younger, but she wanted to keep her privacy and have her best friend live next door.

She hadn't been consulted about anything before her parents made all their decisions. They'd paid more attention to their psychology books than to her feelings. Maybe she'd show them and run away from home. That would serve them right!

Divorce doesn't begin when two people file official papers and appear before a judge to end their marriage. In addition to the legal divorce, couples who separate go through what psychologists call an emotional divorce. Even though marriage is a relationship between two people and the decision to divorce is one they alone make, both legal and emotional divorce involve more than two people. They affect everyone in the family to some extent—especially children. Divorce causes teenagers like Selena, Jeremy, and Bobbi to adjust to major changes in their lives.

The process of emotional divorce, which begins when one or both partners decide they no longer want to continue the relationship, often begins years or months before marriage partners see a lawyer. Sometimes the partners continue to live together in the same house long after their love for each other has ended. Like Selena's mother and father, they may remain married even though they are emotionally distant, because they believe a divorce would hurt their children.

Women who have stayed home to care for children sometimes lack the job skills to support themselves, so they remain married although they no longer care about their partners. Victims of domestic violence may stay in abusive relationships because they are afraid their partners will harm their children or kidnap them if they try to leave.

Other people stay in a marriage when they do not care deeply for their partner because they believe it is easier to do that than to get a legal divorce. The partners may own property jointly or have a business or professional partnership they think would be harmed if they were to go their separate ways. If they aren't looking for a romantic relationship with someone new, they may never file for a legal divorce even though the emotional connection between them is gone. Such relationships are often called marriages of convenience.

The emotional part of divorce doesn't end the day a judge signs the legal decree making the decision final. Even if the legal divorce went quickly and without problems, emotional turmoil that often follows a divorce can be prolonged and painful. Feelings continue to be hurt and tempers may flare for months. Some ex-spouses argue with each other for years after the ink dries on the legal divorce decree.

Making the Decision to Divorce

No two divorces are exactly alike. Sometimes both people make a mutual decision to call an end to their time together as a couple, like Bobbi's parents did. Other times one person chooses to leave the other. Like Selena's father, these people are ready to end the marriage, even though their partners aren't. The person who is left often feels abandoned and must work through grief and rejection toward healing, especially if the divorce has come as a shock.

Marriages end for many reasons. Sometimes two people change and grow apart over time. Their goals, values, and interests simply aren't the same as they were when they got married. While some couples might agree to disagree or work through their differences and remain together, others decide compromise isn't possible. They feel they would be more content either living on their own or in a relationship with another person.

During the years Selena's parents were married, they had drifted apart. Over time they stopped communicating with each other and eventually stopped feeling much of anything for one another. They had become strangers living under one roof. Although neither Selena's mother nor her father were happy together, their lives weren't miserable either. They remained together until Selena's father met a woman he felt deeply about. Only then did he want a divorce.

Other couples divorce because they have conflicts over issues like money, religion, friends, or how household responsibilities should be shared. If they have a difficult time communicating with each other and don't know how to resolve their differences and find solutions, they argue over and over again about the same things. Each time they fight, the anger builds and nothing gets settled.

Jeremy's parents were like that. Even though they joked that they were a classic example of love at first sight and opposites attracting, they had difficulty being together in a long-term relationship. Soon after their marriage, both of them believed that getting married to each other had been a big mistake. The things that had attracted them to each other in the first place became major sources of irritation, but by that time Jeremy's sister had been born.

They argued about everything, from their personalities and values to what brand of toothpaste and laundry soap they should buy and what station they should listen to on the car radio. Even though they tried their best to stay together, as soon as their younger child, Jeremy, was in middle school, they headed for the divorce court.

Sometimes it is difficult to say exactly why the two people who make up a couple decide to go their separate ways. To outsiders, their marriage looks good, but some undefinable chemistry or spark is missing between them. They may simply find each other and the relationship boring.

Bobbi's parents didn't dislike each other, but they didn't want to spend the rest of their lives together. Even though they continued to share many of the same interests, they felt they had fallen out of love with each other, and neither one of them was willing to work to improve the relationship.

Decisions, Decisions

Once marriage partners make the decision that they no longer want to be together, they are faced with choices about their future lifestyle and that of their children. Some of the decisions divorcing parents must make are

- where they and their children will live,
- who will have the primary responsibility for raising the children,
- how much time each parent will spend with the children,
- what arrangements they will make to support two households and meet their children's financial needs, and
- how will they divide their possessions and debts.

Facing so many important decisions at once would be overwhelming to anyone, but for a person feeling sadness, anger, and hurt, trying to make good decisions that affect the whole family can seem impossible. Because marriage partners usually have a history of disagreeing before they decide to divorce, finding choices that both of them agree on takes time and isn't easy even with professional help from a counselor, mediator, or lawyer.

While parents are coming to terms with each other and the future, children often struggle as well. Life can be difficult when you feel that your family is falling apart and you have no idea what the future holds for you because others are calling the shots. Most of the time young children feel anxious when divorcing parents make decisions, but they usually accept the choices that are made for them, because they aren't very independent.

Teenagers, who have come to see their parents as human beings who make mistakes, and who by now have clear ideas about how and where they want to live, aren't always as accepting of the choices that are being made for them.

Selena was furious as she watched her mother throwing her father's things into cardboard boxes, eliminating all reminders of him from the house. If it were up to Selena, she would have left things as they were, waiting for her dad to tire of his girlfriend and move back home. But it wasn't up to her.

Jeremy's parents kept asking him which one of them he wanted to live with and his opinions on the choices they were making, but he soon discovered that they didn't seem to care about his feelings or what he thought he needed. Instead of taking his input to heart, they used what he told them as a weapon in their ongoing battle against each other. Soon he learned it was safer to keep his opinions and his feelings about what was happening to himself.

Bobbi's parents had everything figured out and didn't seem to want or need any feedback from her. She could see the matter-of-fact way they were acting might be right for her brothers because they were too young to understand all that was involved in divorce. Because she was older and more independent than they were, she resented having her mom and dad make all the decisions about her future. She liked her life the way it had always been and didn't want it to change.

The Legal Process

When people marry, they usually do so because they believe they have found that special someone and want to commit to spending the rest of their lives together. Unless they have a great deal of money and make a *pre-nuptial agreement* (a legal contract about how their assets will be divided if the relationship ends), divorce is the last thing on their minds. The wedding ceremony is an expression of their love for one another, and the vows they exchange to cherish and honor each other until death are spoken from the heart.

The government views marriage as a contract between two people, much like a business partnership. In the United States, each state has laws that govern how the legal contract is dissolved when the *parties* (people involved in a legal matter or dispute) who entered into it no longer want to be in the relationship. Although the laws vary somewhat from state to state, they have many similarities.

In general, when a couple decides to split up, they first obtain a legal *separation.* When two people are legally separated, although they are still considered married, they live in different homes and have signed a formal separation agreement that is filed with the court. This agreement divides their financial assets and debts and also outlines who will be responsible for raising the children and who will pay *child support* to take care of their financial needs.

One of the most important and emotional decisions facing many divorcing parents and their children is who will get to live in the family residence or home. Usually this residence goes to the parent the children will live with most of the time. However, because supporting two households is more expensive than when both parents live together—if the residence is a home owned by the family—sometimes it must be sold and both parents move to apartments.

If one parent has a much better job than the other, or one parent worked and moved up the career ladder while the other stayed home and took care of the children, the parent without a job may want *alimony* included in the agreement. Alimony is a monthly payment made by one parent to another to help them get back on their feet financially.

Usually alimony payments are made for a limited time. During that time, the person receiving them is expected to get training or go to school so he or she can eventually get a job and support him- or herself. Occasionally the payments continue until the person who receives them remarries. Alimony is not awarded as frequently as it was in the past, because today both parents often work outside the home.

When both parties to a divorce agree on these choices, they can write up a formal separation agreement themselves and file it with the court. They can also have a lawyer write and file the paperwork for them.

Bobbi's parents didn't face major disagreements about their divorce. Their major conflicts were over how to divide their music collection and their furniture because it included many antiques they'd bought jointly during their time together. It didn't make sense to them to hire a lawyer and go to court over that. Instead, they hired a *mediator* to help solve their disagreements.

A mediator is a neutral person with a good understanding of family law who assists divorcing people to communicate with each other. Mediation helps people cooperate instead of fight. Mediators find out the facts about the family situation and try to understand what each person needs. Next they help people to see different choices they have. Then they help parents compromise on the best options. Even when parents have deeper disagreements than Bobbi's did, mediation usually helps them come up with a separation agreement within weeks.

Mediation is less stressful on parents and children than fighting family battles in divorce court because it helps to resolve conflict. It costs less than hiring lawyers, and it allows families control over decisions that will affect them the rest of their lives, rather than giving that power and control to a judge.

Some couples use legal separation as an opportunity to put off the final decision about whether or not to divorce until later. Separation allows them time to think about whether or not they want to give their relationship another chance. For most couples, however, separation is the first step in filing for divorce.

Many states require a divorcing couple to go through what is called a *waiting period* before a judge reviews the agreement and decrees that the divorce is final. When both parties agree to the terms of the agreement, and acknowledge that they no longer want to be married, their divorce is called *uncontested*.

Uncontested divorces usually move through the court system quickly, sometimes involving only a brief court appearance by one of the parties. On the day of the hearing, the judge takes a few minutes to review the agreement, especially the parts of it that have to do with children, to make sure that their best interests are being protected. He or she may ask the individual or couple a few simple questions to make sure they no longer want to be married. Then the judge signs the divorce decree and the legal part of the marriage is officially ended.

Sometimes only one person wants the divorce. The other person in the marriage is unwilling, emotionally or legally, to let go of the relationship. Other times, no matter how hard they try, parents can't agree to how their belongings should be divided, where the children should live, or how much child support should be paid. They both hire lawyers to argue the two points of view before a judge in order to win what they want. When this happens the divorce is called *contested.*

Contested divorces may take many months or years to move through the court system, especially if couples, acting out of anger, use lawyers to get back at one another. While their parents are doing legal battle, children feel stress, not only from their parents' anger, but from their uncertainty about the future during the legal battle. Until the judge makes his or her decision, their future remains up in the air.

In Canada, a law called the Divorce Act regulates how divorces are granted. In order to obtain a divorce, people must prove that a partner has committed adultery (had sexual relations with someone other than the spouse) or has been mentally or physically cruel. Marriage partners may also become divorced by living apart from each other for at least a year. Most Canadians who divorce do so by separating, rather than proving the partner has broken the marriage vows. After the judge grants a court decree, it takes effect after 31 days.

Today the legal policy makers in the United States and Canada are beginning to recognize that *adversarial* divorce, in which parents take sides and try to win legal battles, is not good for children. Courts are making attempts to deal with the problems such fighting causes children by requiring divorcing parents to attend educational seminars where they learn the effects of divorce on children. They also learn to spot problems that children with divorcing parents commonly encounter, and they are taught how not to put their children in the middle when they argue. Some courts require children to attend workshops where they learn that their parents' divorce is not their fault, and learn skills to help them cope with this difficult time in their lives.

Child Custody

Because it changes the relationship of children to one or both parents, custody is the divorce decision that has the most impact on children and young adults. In addition to *physical custody* (which parent the children will live with), *legal custody* must be decided. Legal custody indicates who will make decisions about the child's education, religion, and other important areas of life.

Most of the time, parents decide who will have custody of the children. Custody arrangements are worked out differently in different families. When Selena's parents divorced, there was no question that she would live with her mother—her father's new lifestyle left little room for her. Bobbi's parents decided to continue sharing the responsibility of caring for their children.

Jeremy's parents kept fighting over their children after their divorce, just as they had when they were married. When, like Jeremy's mom and dad, parents cannot cooperate and do not want to mediate, a judge determines which parent will get child custody.

Child custody disputes are usually the only instances that involve children directly in the legal divorce process. When custody is decided by the courts, young people who are 12 years old or older are often given a chance to talk to the judge about which parent they want to live with. Even so, that testimony is only one of many factors taken into consideration to reach the final decision about which parent the children will live with.

According to the law in Canada and in every state in the United States, the judge must put the "best interests of the child" first in making his or her decision. In order to gather information necessary to make the best decision, the judge may order a custody evaluation of the children and both parents to be done by psychologists and/or social workers.

In addition to what the children have to say, some of the things a judge takes into consideration are

- the ages of the children and whether they are boys or girls,
- their physical and emotional well-being,
- the physical and emotional health of their parents,
- the lifestyles of both parents, including how stable their home life is,
- the emotional ties between the children and their parents,
- the child's pattern of living up until the divorce,
- how devoted a parent is to the child's best interests, and
- how willing a parent is to make sure the child can maintain a relationship with the other parent.

In the early 1900s when divorces were rare, judges automatically awarded *sole custody* of children to their fathers. Back then, children and women were considered a man's legal property. People also believed that any woman involved in a divorce was morally unfit to care for her children.

By the 1940s and 1950s the trend had reversed itself. Because of a popular belief that mothers had nurturing ability fathers lacked, mothers were automatically given full custody of their children. Courts gave fathers visitation rights and ordered them to pay child support.

Once more, child custody trends are changing. Although today the majority of custody arrangements still give children to the mother, while the father receives the right to spend regularly scheduled time with them, slowly more fathers are gaining custody. In 1992 the number of unmarried fathers who headed single-parent homes was 14 percent, up from 10 percent 12 years before.

Sole custody grants one parent both physical and legal custody of children from the marriage. The parent without custody has the right to visit the child. In the United States this is called *visitation*. In Canada it is called *access*. Sometimes if there is more than one child in the family, a judge might divide custody of the children between the parents. Because most families and most judges don't want to separate brothers and sisters, this arrangement is unusual.

Unfortunately, about a third of all divorced fathers act like Selena's did when he first left her mother, pulling back from their children. Studies show that just under a third of divorced fathers without custody but with visitation rights do not spend time with their children. On the other hand, about three out of 25 divorced fathers without custody continue to see their children once a week.

In time, Selena's father saw her more frequently. When they could finally talk with each other about what had happened, he told her that it had been hard for him to face her and that he'd believed she might adjust more quickly if he kept his distance. Later he explained to her, too, how much he missed being around her. "It hurt too much," he said. "I thought if I didn't see you, I'd get over missing you, but it didn't work that way. I couldn't forget my daughter."

Unlike the past, today more and more fathers and mothers are asking judges to award custody of their children to both of them—the arrangement that Bobbi's parents worked out for their family. This type of custody is called *joint* or *shared custody*.

When parents are given *joint physical custody* of their children, the children spend about an equal amount of time with their mother and their father. When parents have *joint legal custody,* both of them share equally in making medical, educational, and religious decisions about their children's lives, even though the children may spend most of their time with one parent. Courts in most states routinely award joint legal custody. In New Mexico and New Hampshire, the courts *must* award joint custody unless it would endanger the children's best interest or the parents' health and safety. Some states allow judges to award joint custody when one parent doesn't want it, but only about half of them are willing to give parents joint physical custody unless both parents want it and they are able to work together. They must be able to communicate with each other in a way that will be good for their children.

In some divorces, parents ask for and are awarded both joint physical and legal custody. The advantage of sharing joint legal and physical custody is that children get to be with and know both parents. In addition to maintaining contact with their children, both parents have more free time to do things they want.

Parents with joint custody have to work out living arrangements for the children based on their schedules and where they live. When divorced parents live relatively close to each other, children can spend alternative weeks or months at the parents' respective homes. Sometimes, when distance is involved, they spend alternate years. If the plans force a child to change schools, the parents may agree that the child will spend weekdays with one parent and weekends, holidays and summer vacations with the other.

When parents don't agree on the schedules, the judge or mediator will make a plan for them and make certain they stick to it. Only in rare instances do the children remain in the family's home while the parents move in and out according to the judge's schedule. This living arrangement is sometimes called *birds' nest custody*.

Occasionally neither parent can or is willing to take responsibility for the children. Sometimes this happens because both parents use drugs, or they drink, or have severe emotional problems. When this is the case, child custody may be awarded to another relative like a grandparent, or children may be placed in a foster home where they will be cared for.

Canadian courts treat custody much the same as United States courts. In Canada, because the waiting period between the separation and divorce is so long, parents can apply to the courts for an interim custody decree. The judge usually decides which parent will have interim custody of the children on the basis of *affidavits,* sworn statements by the parents. Because interim custody is meant to be temporary, it lasts until the divorce decree becomes final.

Visitation

Even when a judge grants one parent sole physical custody, children need continuing relationships with both parents. For this reason, most divorce decrees give *visitation rights* that guarantee that a non-custodial parent can spend time with his or her children. Usually parents work out the details of visitation in the separation agreement.

Many families have an arrangement that allows children to spend alternating weekends with the parent they do not live with. The children can also visit several hours on a weeknight during the week when they spend the weekend with their custodial parent. Usually special holidays, like birthdays, are alternated or shared.

Courts usually order that visitation will occur at reasonable times and places so that both the parents' and their children's schedules are taken into account. The schedule might be changed if one or more of the children are ill, the parent is ill, work schedules change, or a parent moves to another town.

When the details are left to the parents to work out, they need to communicate and cooperate for the visits to go smoothly. If they can't, the judge may set up a fixed schedule.

Jeremy's parents argued with each other, angrily cancelling and rescheduling visits, until a court-appointed social worker helped them make a timetable. After Jeremy's dad came into his mom's house without knocking, raided the refrigerator and criticized her because Jeremy wasn't ready, although he'd arrived two hours before he said he would, the social worker told him he needed to pick the children up at a neutral place. He also informed Jeremy's mom that she would be in contempt of court if she tried to get back at her ex-husband by keeping him from seeing his children as she'd threatened to do.

It was decided that every Saturday morning at eight sharp Jeremy's mom would bring him and his sister to a coffee shop about halfway between the two houses, where his father would pick them up. At first the arrangement felt strange, but later on, he got used to it, especially when his dad began buying breakfast for them after his mom left. Maybe his family didn't handle visits like his friends' families did, but he felt better about it than the old way with all the accusations and hollering.

Often as children grow older, they want more say in how often and when they will visit the parent who no longer lives in the same house they do. When Jeremy began feeling bad because he never got to spend any time alone with his dad, his parents, who by this time were able to talk with each other a little more calmly, responded by changing the visitation schedule so that each child would have one day to be alone with him every two months.

Judges deny parental visitation or access for very few reasons. The courts do not stop a parent from spending time with a child just because a child is angry at the parent who has moved out of the family home, decides they are "bad," and refuses to see them. Neither are visits denied simply because one parent is angry at the other one. Even when a parent does not make court-ordered child support payments or pays them late, visitation still must continue. Finally, parents who are in a new romantic relationship are not forbidden from seeing their children as long as sexual acts do not involve children and are not conducted in front of them.

Eventually Selena's father began inviting her to spend the night at his house. Selena didn't like his girlfriend, and now, instead of blaming her mother, she blamed this woman for breaking up her family. Besides, when she thought about all the hurt her mother had felt, she felt disloyal when she was even polite to this woman her father said would be her new stepmother someday.

When she returned home, she complained to her mom about the living arrangement and told her she didn't want to stay in the same house with her father's girlfriend. Angry, her mother called her lawyer and demanded that he ask the judge to stop her daughter's visitation with her father. The lawyer told her that, in a situation like this, most judges order that the visits continue. "We could go to court and try, but it would cost more money than it is worth," he said and he suggested that Selena's mom see a counselor to work on getting over her feelings of jealousy.

Today courts usually do not deny parents the right to spend time with their children because of sexual orientation. In the past it was different, but attitudes are changing. The fact that a mother or father prefers romantic partners of the same sex is not reason enough to stop a child from having contact with a mother or father, either through custody or visitation.

Now Pennsylvania, New Mexico, the District of Columbia, California, and Alaska all have laws that forbid judges to deny a parent custody or visitation just because she or he is lesbian or gay. Sometimes, however, judges in those and other states deny custody and visitation to lesbian and gay parents because of their own prejudices, or how homosexuality is viewed in the community. When this happens, the parent who is denied visitation can appeal the judge's decision.

Visits are stopped or limited for very few reasons. If a parent has a problem like alcoholism or mental illness that causes instability and inability to provide a good environment for the child, a judge may deny that person visitation rights. The same will happen if a parent has been violently physically abusive to children or has sexually molested them. If a parent has been convicted of a major crime, visitation will sometimes be denied.

In instances like these, a judge may not forbid a non-custodial parent to see a child entirely, but will order that visitations be supervised for the protection of the child. For example, a judge might order *supervised visitation* if he or she has reason to believe the non-custodial parent might kidnap the child. During supervised visits, another adult besides the custodial parent is present at all times. That person is usually a court-appointed social worker. In other instances, the court might appoint a family friend or a relative.

Child Support

Child support, payments made by one parent to the other, help meet the children's need for housing, food, an education, and medical care. The amount of money a parent is ordered to pay depends on several things.

In 1988, the United States Congress passed a law establishing uniform child support guidelines to make sure the decision would be made fairly throughout the country. According to this law, the amount of child support a parent must pay is worked out by considering

- the earnings and financial needs of the parents,
- the earnings, income, and financial resources of each child,
- the ages of the children, and
- the physical and educational needs of the children.

Canada has a similar law.

Once a monthly amount is decided upon, the parent who is ordered to pay child support either pays the money directly to the custodial parent or to the court, which then issues a check to the custodial parent. If circumstances change, such as a parent's losing a job or a child's needing to be placed in a special school that charges tuition, parents can take the order before a judge to have it modified to fit the changing family needs.

Jeremy was excited to hear that his father was paying $300 a month in child support, but when his mother began getting the money, he never saw a dime of it. Whenever he asked her for money, she told him she'd spent it on the electricity bill or at the grocery store. It seemed to him that he should be getting child support. He knew what he wanted to spend it on—new clothes and CDs. Even his dad said it was his right to spend it however he wanted to.

Many teenagers are under the false impression that child support is much the same as an allowance, as Jeremy was. They think they are old enough to manage the money, so it should be paid to them. Because child support is meant to help cover the costs of maintaining a household for the children, it is paid to the parent, not the child or the young adult. According to law, it is up to the custodial parent, not the child, to determine how the money will be spent.

Once all of the decisions have been made and reviewed by a judge, the divorce decree is signed and legally the marriage is over. The family is not. Even though a man and a woman may decide to end their relationship through divorce, they are still deeply connected to their children. Through their children, they will always have some connection to each other, even though it has changed.

Legal divorce marks the end of a way of life family members are accustomed to. It changes what is called a *nuclear family*—a mother, father, and their children living in one home—to a *bi-nuclear family*—a mother living in one home, a father in another, and the children moving between the two.

At the same time divorce is an ending, it is a beginning with a whole new set of challenges and choices for parents and their children.

2

Surviving the Stress

When families are filled with continuous conflict, is breaking up better for parents and their children than living in a house that has become a battle zone? Or should parents try to stay together at all costs so that their children can grow up in the family into which they were born?

Parents, children, and even the experts who study how family members cope with divorce, don't always agree about the effects marriage break-ups have on children. Some people, because of their religious or moral values, believe that divorce is always a bad thing, and that laws should be passed making it more difficult to end a marriage. Others feel that the individual happiness and opportunity for personal growth of marriage partners is much more important than keeping a family unit together.

Most people's viewpoints fall in the middle of these two extremes. They have mixed feelings, and sometimes hurt feelings, about divorce. Because divorce is usually a time of conflicts, loss, and broken trust, divorce is a difficult thing to feel good about even when it seems to be the best choice for parents and their children.

When two people have tried repeatedly to make a go of the relationship and they can't, or when one of them tries and the other refuses, there is little to be done to keep the marriage together. In that case, most people see divorce as a necessary evil—something they don't like, but something they can't stop from happening. They hope that in the long run the decision to end the marriage will improve their lives and those of their children.

Many people hold one set of beliefs about divorce in general but find that they feel differently when it happens in their family. Take a few minutes to think about how you feel about divorce in general, and how you would feel if it were closer to home. What reasons do you think couples should have to end their marriage? Do you believe it is better for a person to stay married to someone no longer loved so that children can live with both parents, or do you believe that children are better off living in a single-parent home than one in which their parents no longer care about one another or get along? Should the children's ages matter in the decision to divorce?

No matter how teenagers feel about divorce, when parents choose to end their marriage, most of the time they and their brothers and sisters have no say in that decision. They might disagree with the choice, but for them it is a fact of life—one they must accept and make the best of because the situation is out of their control. In order to survive this stressful time, they need to work through the loss that divorce brings into their lives and adapt to the changes that face them.

Broken Homes, Broken Lives?

After Bobbi's mom and dad announced their decision to end their marriage, she started noticing how often the subject was mentioned on television, in the paper, and in conversations. She was surprised at the number of times she heard the words: *broken homes* and *single-parent families.* More often than not, when she heard people using those words they followed them with stories of crime and poverty, drug abuse or mental illness.

At first she shrugged her shoulders and told herself that it was other families of divorce being discussed, not hers. Later on, as she started struggling to cope with the changes her parents had imposed on her life and with her feelings about what was happening, she began to wonder if maybe the television reporters and news writers weren't talking about her and her brothers, too.

Her uneasiness about the future wasn't helped by the way her grandparents began acting. Her dad's parents, who belonged to a conservative church, seemed ashamed. Their visits grew fewer and fewer. When she did see them, they acted distant, as if their granddaughter were part of something so embarrassing and bad that just being around her made them uncomfortable.

Her mom's parents, who still called her their grandbaby, kept asking her if she was all right, and when they mentioned her parents' divorce, their voices were filled with pity. One time she overheard her grandma say to her mom: "I'm heartbroken for the children. This is such a horrible thing you two are putting those poor babies through. I don't see how you could do it to them."

Despite her parents' reassurances, as the days went on Bobbi's discomfort mounted to the point that she started closely watching her younger brothers for signs of mental illness. She looked for signs in herself as well. Would she be okay or would she drop out of school, start using drugs, get pregnant, and face problems all her life simply because her parents had stacked the deck against her by filing for divorce?

Researchers who study how well children do after their parents' divorce tell us that all of them, no matter what their ages, experience emotional pain afterward. Feeling that way is no fun, but it *is* normal. Sometimes the emotional turmoil teenagers experience because of all the changes in their lives can be so overwhelming that they feel like they are going to go haywire. Trying to grow into adulthood and getting ready to leave home in a few years is tough enough without having to go through all these things. Living through their parents' divorce just doesn't seem fair.

It *isn't* fair. The good news is that it isn't forever. In time the difficult feelings ease up and the changes faced by children of divorce usually don't seem so impossible to cope with. Years of research show that even though some children and young adults whose parents divorce have a more difficult time than others, all children of divorce are not doomed to suffer lives of hardship and emotional torment, as Bobbi feared.

Some children of divorce do face major struggles with the difficulties divorce throws their way. Psychologist Judith Wallerstein, who wrote *Second Chances: Men, Women and Children a Decade After Divorce* based on a study of 130 children whose parents had divorced, found that most of them experienced the divorce as "devastating and wrenching." In 1989 Dr. Wallerstein wrote that their negative feelings lasted, to at least some degree, for about 15 years. Even when they seemed to have adjusted to their parents' divorce, the feelings resurfaced when they became teenagers. She and other divorce experts believe that this recycling might be triggered by young people's interest in forming romantic relationships. As they begin dating, the anger, sadness, and fear of abandonment that they felt at the time of the divorce come back and must be worked through again.

Researchers William Axinn, an associate professor of sociology at Pennsylvania State University, and Arlin Thornton, professor of sociology and research scientist with the Survey Research Center at the University of Michigan, looked at the long-term consequences of parents' divorces on their children's adult relationships. After studying for 18 years children of divorce in Detroit, they found that some children whose parents divorced grew up disillusioned with marriage, especially if their mother didn't remarry. As adults they often lived with their partner rather than marrying and had fewer children than did other people. Those who married tended to do so at a later age than their friends did. Adults whose parents had divorced also tended to be more tolerant of the option of divorce than other people were. Despite these attitudes about marriage, the research did not show that their relationships were unhappy ones.

Other studies paint a much brighter picture of the future of children of divorce. They seem to show that most children whose parents' marriages break up learn to cope quite well. University of Virginia psychologist Mavis Hetherington's study of over 1,500 children of divorce—more than ten times the number of children studied by Dr. Wallerstein—is one of them. She found that 80 percent of the children she studied over the past 25 years grew up to be well adjusted. Although they looked back to the time of their parents' divorce as one of the most painful in their lives, that pain usually lasted for only a year or two.

Twenty percent of the children she studied experienced severe problems at some time in their lives, about twice as many as children from intact families. Some of the difficulties they encountered were dropping out of school, depression, and unstable relationships. Alcohol or drug use is another problem that other researchers have found some children whose parents have divorced face in their lives.

The reasons that some young people have a more difficult time after their parents' marriage breaks up than other teenagers with divorced parents do are many. In the first place, divorces are different. Some come after years of bitter fighting, like the way it was in Jeremy's family. Others arrive as a total surprise, sending shock waves through the family as Selena's parents' divorce did. Some divorces proceed smoothly because both partners want them. Others are marked by fighting every step of the way, with children being drawn into the arguments.

Families have different ways of coping with the stress of divorce, and individuals within families have their own unique ways of coping, too. Some people have an easy time figuring out what emotions they are feeling, and then expressing them in positive ways. Others have difficulty knowing how they feel, let alone talking about it with others and asking for what they want or need.

The studies on children of divorce that have been done so far indicate that a number of circumstances influence the emotional impact divorce has on them. In general, children and young adults have a more difficult time both during and after their parents' divorce when their family life before the divorce was not healthy.

Some families are more functional, or seem to work better, than others. Family members have good communication and problem-solving skills. They respect one anothers' needs and wishes and, at the same time, learn to take responsibility for their own feelings and actions. Children from families such as these are encouraged to develop their own talents and are taught to make their own decisions. Parents provide their children guidance, support, and discipline.

Because they are told and shown how much they are loved, young adults who have grown up in healthy families tend to approach life with confidence and a positive attitude. They develop high levels of self-esteem, which enable them to endure stressful events going on around them without falling apart.

In addition, they are encouraged by their parents to have interests and friendships outside of the family. Since they have learned to care about themselves, they form connections with other people, so they are not totally dependent on their family for love and emotional nurturing. If Mom or Dad is unavailable, they can get what they need from other people in their lives.

Other young adults aren't so fortunate. Problems such as chemical dependency, incest, mental illness, and spouse or child abuse consume every family member's time and attention. Families like these that don't work well are called *dysfunctional families*. Parents and children are all so focused on the family problem that they have little time to think about how they feel or what they want and need. They are so busy caring for the family member or members with the problem, they don't have any energy left to care for themselves.

Children raised in families where one or more people have major problems they haven't gotten help for, learn at an early age to hide their feelings from themselves and not to talk about them when they do surface—especially not to outsiders. Oftentimes they learn, as well, to pretend the family problem isn't there. They may be so caught up in covering up that they don't have support networks in the form of friends, relatives in their extended families, or teachers they trust.

Not all dysfunctional families have a member or members with obviously severe problems. Some adults simply lack the parenting skills to provide the emotional nurturing, guidance, and discipline their children need. Perhaps their own parents weren't very good at raising children, or neglected or abused them. Maybe because their parents died or abandoned them at an early age, they never learned how to provide a healthy home life for their own children. For whatever reason, they simply can't give their children what they need for an emotionally positive and stable family life.

Children who come from troubled families often start developing problems long before their parents divorce, according to researcher Andrew Churlin of Johns Hopkins University. Divorce is one of many difficult things that has happened in their lives and doesn't necessarily cause teenagers' grades to drop, or impel them to start shoplifting.

Just as all parents aren't alike in their parenting ability, no two teenagers are alike. Those who have previously developed a number of coping skills and have an adequate support system in place, tend to adapt to the aftermath of divorce without major difficulties. Other teens have tremendous problems accepting the fact that their parents are divorcing and may experience major difficulties at school, with friends, and at home, after their parents' marriage breaks up.

In general, teenagers have an easier time coping with their parents' divorce when:

The parent they live with does not have an extremely difficult time adjusting to the divorce. How parents handle their divorce affects the way their children will adjust to what is going on in their lives. Some parents react well. They acknowledge their unhappiness and their stress, but they are committed to building new lives for themselves and their children, so they work through it.

These parents take the time to talk to their children, reassuring them that they love them and that eventually life will smooth out. They let their children know that the divorce is not their fault and that they will always be there for their children—both to listen to their feelings and to let them know what is going on. They do their best to create a secure environment for their children.

When they need help getting themselves together, parents with good coping skills seek emotional support from friends or therapists, not from their children. They do not expect their children to listen to tirades about the other parent or ask their children for advice about personal matters. When their children need help they cannot provide in adjusting to the divorce, they find ways to obtain it. Other parents are too caught up in their own fear, sadness, and anger, to pay attention to their children's needs.

When Selena's father left, her mother not only felt upset by his demand for a divorce, but once again she experienced old feelings from when her father, Selena's grandfather, died. She had never grieved for him. Instead she ignored her feelings and tried to go on with her life as if nothing had happened. This new loss made her pain seem unbearable. Although she knew she shouldn't be burdening her daughter with all the inner struggles she was going through, she felt like she couldn't help it.

The situation worsened when she started going through what she called "the divorce crazies." She began drinking to try to escape the pain she was feeling. At first it was just a little bit, a few glasses of wine in the afternoon. She said it gave her courage to get through the day and helped her to sleep at night. Soon a little became a little more, and the more she drank, the more it seemed she ignored her children.

It was as if she were living in her own little world, and Selena felt abandoned. She certainly couldn't look to her mom as a role model, or to provide her with suggestions about how to cope with all the changes in her life, because her mother wasn't coping with them. Since Selena didn't feel she could depend on her mother for emotional support, she didn't know where to turn.

Young people in her situation not only worry about the divorce and how it will affect them, they worry about what will happen to their parent. Often they feel an obligation to take charge of the family and often act like they are the adult and their parent is the child as they try to offer comfort and keep the home running.

The children get to spend time with both parents. Ideally children and young adults need to spend time with both parents, even though they may no longer all live in one household. Eleanor Maccoby, a researcher from Stanford University who studied over 1,000 families, found that when parents could *co-parent* (take joint responsibility for their children), joint custody was the best arrangement for children because it insured that both parents would continue to play an important part in their children's lives. If the parents' arguing made that arrangement impossible, she said in an interview on National Public Radio, continued involvement of both parents in a child's life through visitation was necessary in order for children to get their own lives back on track after divorce.

Co-parenting isn't always easy, but it is so important that the Children's Rights Council, a national, nonprofit organization, was formed in 1985 to insure that children of divorce have frequent, meaningful, and continuing contact with both parents and with extended family members, such as aunts and uncles and grandparents, even though their parents' marriage has ended. The advocacy group has come up with a bill of rights for children that includes not only the right to have contact with both parents, but the right to know the reason for not having contact if it is denied.

Florida, one of the states with a policy encouraging shared parental responsibility, has a law that orders each divorced parent to promote a good relationship between the children and the other parent. This includes a child's free access to both parents. By law parents cannot do anything to interfere with the children's love and respect for the other parent. Both parents have to encourage and enable communication between the children and the other parent in person, on the telephone, and through the mail, or they break the law.

Continuing to spend time with both parents is important because when contact is drastically cut down or completely cut off, children and young adults often feel abandoned and rejected. Their self-esteem plummets. Like Selena, they may mistakenly believe that the parent they no longer see has stopped loving them. Even though children might understand that the parent who has moved away from the home in which they live still cares about them, they may feel depressed and blame themselves for the lack of contact.

They receive love and approval from both parents. There is much more to being a parent than just spending time with a child. Ann Peterson, a psychologist from the National Science Foundation who did research with teenagers, found that young adults who have good relationships with both parents after a divorce, do better in their own lives than those who have a good relationship with only one parent.

Bobbi saw her father often because he and her mom shared custody of her and her brothers. Whenever she was at his house, he always seemed preoccupied with other things than his children. He brought work home with him and when he did plan an activity with her, it was always something like watching videos or going to a movie. They never seemed to talk. Even though she got to see her dad, sometimes she wondered if her father really wanted her around. Maybe he was just sharing custody of his children with her mom because he felt obligated to do so.

Fortunately for Bobbi, her dad's escape into his work was a temporary way in which he tried to numb some of the emotional pain he felt because he no longer lived with his children full-time. He was afraid to let himself be emotionally close to his children, because then it would make him feel even sadder than he already did when it came time to say good-bye to them for a few days. In time, he was able to relax around his children and allow himself to enjoy the time he spent with them instead of thinking ahead to the moment he would have to drive them back to their mom's house.

Another reason he held himself emotionally distant from his children was that he had a hard time with his feelings about the decision to end his marriage to Bobbi's mother. Some days he felt guilty at wanting his freedom. Other days, he was angry at his ex-wife for not understanding him and not wanting the same things out of life that he did. He had moments when he thought he'd made a mistake in getting a divorce but that it was too late to go back and undo what had been done. As he went through all this turmoil, he feared saying or doing the wrong thing when his children were around. When he acted stiff and self-conscious, it wasn't because he didn't like his kids; he was preoccupied with what he was going through, and he didn't want to put his children through any more than they were already enduring.

Other parents have difficulty relating to their children after divorce because they simply aren't used to being nurturing or openly expressing the love they feel for them. They weren't very involved in raising their children during the marriage and they don't have a history of spending time with them. They may not really know their children and fear the role that is now expected of them.

Selena's father was like that. He thought about spending time with her, but he didn't have any idea of what to talk about with her or what to do. Throughout his marriage to Selena's mom, he hadn't been the one to take care of Selena when she was sick, to amuse her when she was stuck inside the house during winter storms, or to discipline her when she misbehaved. When he was given visitation rights, he was so overwhelmed that he stayed away from his daughter, then later tried to push his new girlfriend into the role of parent.

Feeling pushed away by or cut off from a parent causes troubling feelings for all young people, but girls, especially, have a difficult time when it happens. In a study of young women whose parents had divorced and whose contact with their fathers was cut back or ended completely, researcher Neil Kalter found that they had lower self-esteem. They also showed more "delinquent-like" behavior and more difficulty with having gratifying, lasting relationships with members of the opposite sex when they grew up than did girls whose parents remained married.

Based on the results of his study, Kalter concluded that sometimes girls believe their father has rejected them because they aren't pretty, bright, or athletic enough for him to want to be around them. Without frequent loving contact from a father, a girl's sense of herself as a woman suffers.

Divorcing parents are able to keep their conflicts to a reasonable level and leave their children out of their arguments. On the whole, psychological research reveals that the level of anger and conflict between divorcing parents is probably the most important factor in their children's adjustment to divorce. Studies show that parents who are in touch with their own feelings and those who can manage conflicts in a healthy way, agreeing to disagree without drawing their children into their break-up battles, make divorce easier for their children.

In research by Constance R. Ahrons on families who had recently experienced divorce about half of the families were able to have what she called a "good divorce"—one where conflict was kept to a minimum and children were kept out of the disagreements. The parents were able to work as a team to raise their children, even though they disagreed about certain issues and had chosen to end their marriages.

Children from families where parents argue often may actually be better off after the divorce, once parents "unhook" from each other and the conflicts that keep them fighting, according to researcher Paul Amato of the University of Nebraska. Until they disengage and call a halt to the emotional boxing matches, however, parents make life very difficult for their children.

Jeremy saw his dad quite often, but much of their time together was taken up as his father picked for information about his mom's activities and criticizing the way she was raising Jeremy and his sister. He wanted to talk to his father, not his mom, about how he was doing in sports, and his problems with his math teacher. The situation at home wasn't much better—the kindest thing his mother could manage to say about his father was that he was a loser and a no-good bum. Jeremy couldn't help but feel that when his mother criticized his father that she was really saying bad things about him, too.

He should have been used to it by now, because his home life had never been peaceful, Jeremy thought, but their behavior made him angry. The way they both acted caused him to think sometimes that *he* should see a lawyer and get a divorce from both of them.

Because conflicts that can't easily be resolved cause couples to break up in the first place, no divorce is completely friendly. If parents had that great a relationship, they would be happy together, not getting divorced. The level of conflict people have with each other has more to do with how they handle anger than the actual issues they disagree on.

About the only way Jeremy's parents related to each other was through arguing. They were angry at each other, but much of their anger didn't have anything to do with the situation. Instead, it came from the fact that both of them were raised in families where there had been physical and emotional violence. Their rage at the verbal abuse and the slaps and beatings that they had endured as children was always at a simmering point. During the time they were together, they let off steam by bickering with one another. Their reactions to one another were so automatic, they didn't even think that there might be another way to resolve their differences.

Some people use anger to cover emotions such as sadness, guilt, or abandonment. Feeling outraged and going on the attack allows them to focus on how bad they believe the other person is and how terrible their actions are, instead of looking at themselves. Rather than letting themselves feel their own emotional pain and work through it, they distract themselves by lashing out, and trying to get back at, or hurt the person they believe has wronged them.

People who have a difficult time expressing their anger appropriately when they feel it, store it up inside of themselves. Over days and months and years their resentments build. Minor irritations over things like someone eating the last of the ice cream, or forgetting to turn the lights off, can grow into huge conflicts if they aren't handled at the time.

A parent who has been silent for years can suddenly start acting like a Tasmanian devil as all the rage comes pouring out—often inappropriately. Very few of us would yell at people and call them names because they ate the last of the chocolate ripple ice cream five years ago. That wouldn't make sense.

Think about a time when something another person did made you feel angry, but you didn't say anything about it. You may have acted as if nothing was wrong, but chances are, over time, you remembered your anger, and maybe even collected more, until you may have expressed it in a way that the other person and even you didn't expect.

When anger that has been suppressed for a long period of time starts coming out, a parent may react to an irritation in the present, like the other parent's being ten minutes late to pick the children up for visitation, with an inappropriate degree of hostility. In simpler terms, that parent has a temper tantrum. Or those who denied their feelings may turn the one they are angry with into an enemy, convincing themselves that the enemy has absolutely no good qualities.

The very first right of children of divorce on the Children's Rights Council's bill of rights is the most important one: "The right to be treated as important human beings, with unique feelings, ideas and desires, and not as a source of argument between parents." Because divorced parents remain connected through their children, fighting over them is often a tempting way to express the anger they feel toward one another over completely different matters.

Angry parents who don't communicate their feelings directly to each other often draw their children into the middle of the all-out war they have declared against one another, even using them as weapons. Some of the ways they do this are

- insisting that young people take sides,
- telling them things about the other parent they have no business knowing,

- using them as spies in order to gather information about what the other parent is doing,
- playing "he said/she said" by getting children to carry messages back and forth instead of communicating directly,
- fighting over custody or withholding visitation as a way to get back at the other parent,
- competing with each other by trying to "buy" love and attention or refusing to set limits on childrens' behavior,
- trying to make children feel sorry for them by using the divorce and the other parent as an excuse for everything that is wrong in their lives,
- telling a young person,"You're just like your dad/mother," and intending it as an insult.

The divorce doesn't cause too many major changes in the children's lives. Children whose parents are divorcing sometimes fear that the parental split spells an end to their family. Most of the time this belief is not based on reality. In reality, the family takes a different shape, becoming a bi-nuclear family rather than a nuclear one. Even when a parent abandons the family and cuts all contact with the children, the family then becomes a single-parent family—different from a two-parent household, but a family just the same. Even though it is a family, it is changed by divorce.

Adapting to any sort of change is a stressful process because you can only guess, but you don't know for sure, what will happen next. Although change helps us to grow, until we get used to the new circumstances life has brought us, our sense of security and safety are gone. This is true for positive changes, like winning the lottery, as well as those we view as negative, like divorce.

Young adults, even those in families where parents are not going through a divorce, are faced with a number of changes as their bodies mature and they gain more independence in preparation for leaving home and living on their own some day. Take a few minutes to think back to how your life was when you were a child in elementary school, and compare that with how it is now. What are some of the changes that have come about just as a result of growing up?

Even though many parts of life remain the same, the changing shape of a family experiencing divorce brings changes in lifestyle that directly affect teenagers and younger children—and causes more stress as well. Whether parents have decided on sole or shared custody, most teens find themselves shuttling between two households. Even when custody and visitation arrangements work smoothly, these different households often come with different expectations and rules so that teenagers must learn to adjust to constant change.

Jeremy's father was an orderly person who wanted everything in his apartment to be neat. He didn't like it when his son left video game cartridges strewn over the living-room floor and didn't make his bed in the morning. On the other hand, he didn't care how long his son talked on the telephone and didn't say anything if he showered until the hot water ran out on the weekends he stayed there. Jeremy's mother was just the opposite about those particular things. Untidiness didn't faze her a bit, but she went ballistic if her son tied up the phone or used too much hot water.

At first it was hard for him to adjust when he went back and forth. No matter how hard he tried, he forgot the rules sometimes. Neither his mom or his dad seemed to understand how hard it was for him to adapt to their ways of doing things that were different from how life had been when they shared the same home. They acted like he was deliberately trying to get at them, when in truth, he was having a very hard time adjusting.

After Bobbi's father moved to his own apartment, she began spending three days a week with him. Even though she had her own bedroom and many of her clothes and books and tapes at her dad's house, it always seemed that when she was there, she needed something she'd left at her mom's. When she was at her mother's house, she missed the things she'd left at her dad's. Instead of feeling like she belonged in two places, she felt like she didn't belong anywhere until she got used to this new way of living.

Being a member of two households can put a crimp in the time young people have to spend with their friends and on social activities of their own choosing. This is especially true when it involves a move across town or even across the country. Moving brings even more changes—a different school and the sometimes scary task of making new friends. If the young person remains where he or she has always lived, but a divorced parent moves out of the area, it is a challenge to maintain a close relationship with the long-distance parent.

Living in a single-parent home is different than living where two parents are present. Because single parents have so much to do and so little time to do it, they may ask their teenagers to take on more household responsibilities and to be more independent than they were in the past. If a parent who formerly stayed home now works, daily routines can change radically.

When Selena thought about it, her life before her parents got divorced seemed carefree. When her father left and her mother went to work in addition to taking college classes, all that changed. After school, she couldn't hang out with her friends anymore. Instead she had to come straight home to get dinner started. Her mom no longer had time to iron or even do her laundry for her. When she did have time to hang out, she didn't have money for soda or movies like she'd had before. Instead of buying her lunch at school, she had to bring a sandwich from home—one she'd made herself because that was her job, too, making school lunches.

Many teenagers like Selena, whose parents divorce, experience changes in their lifestyles because suddenly their parents lack the financial resources to keep living the way they did in the past. Because divorced parents live in two households, rather than living in one and sharing their resources, essentials like rent and utilities take more money.

Unless divorcing parents are wealthy and have money to spare, their children often have to give up things they were used to having before the divorce. Sometimes those things are not so difficult to live without, like cable television or eating out at restaurants three nights a week. Other things are harder. Jeremy, who lived to play basketball during the season, was very upset when his parents couldn't afford to buy the shoes he needed for the sport. He thought about getting a part-time job, but that would mean missing practice and getting kicked off the team. Luckily, his grandparents came through for him with the money he needed, but the experience really made him think about how much things had changed because of the divorce.

Financial difficulties are made worse when a parent stops making child support payments. In the United States, many single-parent families live at or below the poverty level. Although not having enough money does not in and of itself ruin people's lives, poverty makes life very difficult and raises the risk of dropping out of school, getting in trouble with the law, and substance abuse.

Selena's mom received her check for less than a year before Selena's dad remarried and stopped sending money to her. Instead, he occasionally bought clothes or presents. Whenever she visited him, he took her out to eat and to the arcade. Selena liked those times, but when her mom's car broke down, there was no money to fix it. And even though her mother continued to work while she was going to school, they had to move to a neighborhood where rents were lower and crime was higher in order to afford a place to live.

Her mom explained to her that these changes were temporary. As soon as she got her degree and was able to get a better-paying job, things would smooth out financially. In the meantime, she would apply for Aid to Families with Dependent Children, and because of the Uniform Child Support Act, the government would take the responsibility of trying to collect the child support Selena's dad owed.

The Effects of Stress

When divorce turns people's lives temporarily upside down, stress can cause them to have some sleepless nights, forget things they would normally remember, lose their appetites, and even have bad dreams. Those things are perfectly normal. Tossing and turning some nights, or forgetting where you put your homework, may be unpleasant, but when they happen only occasionally, you are still able to keep going on with your life. You go to school, relate to people in your family, and keep your friends, even though once in a while you might be a bit more irritable with them than usual. Most young adults find that these stress effects lessen in time as they start adjusting to their parents' divorce.

Other children of divorce have so much going on in their lives that they get overwhelmed to the point of finding it impossible to function in their daily lives. A few weeks after her parents divorced, Selena started getting stomachaches and headaches. She felt hopeless, as if her life was never going to get better, and she cried often. One day, when she thought about her dad and what he was doing, she burst into tears right in the middle of biology class. She started worrying about everything, including herself and how she was reacting to her parents' divorce.

When young adults lose friends, can't relate to family members, or get into trouble at school following their parents' divorce, it is an indication they may have developed what mental health professionals call an *adjustment disorder.* Some signals that a young adult is having an unusually difficult time adjusting to the changes his or her parents' divorce is causing are

- pulling back from friends and isolating him- or herself,
- picking fights with friends,
- having headaches and stomachaches,
- feeling angry at one or both parents
- skipping school,
- getting bad grades,
- losing sleep,
- having mood swings,
- stealing,
- using alcohol or drugs, or
- developing poor eating habits or eating disorders.

Younger children with an adjustment disorder have different symptoms. They might start having temper tantrums, wet the bed, or wake up at night screaming in fright from nightmares. Sometimes they regress, "forgetting" certain thing they have learned like how to talk, or living without diapers.

When these symptoms start within three months of the major life change and continue six months or longer, the person who has them needs to seek professional help to get life back on the right track. Left alone, adjustment disorders caused by stress can cause depression.

A good place to start seeking help when teenagers are feeling overwhelmed is to talk with parents. If they don't respond to the concerns, making an appointment with a school counselor to discuss problems is a good idea. When counselors can't provide the kind of assistance needed, they can refer young people to other sources of help. Some of them are listed at the end of this book. If you need to talk to someone about what you're feeling right away and can't wait for an appointment, you can call a crisis hot line for emotional support and referrals to others who can help (see chapter 7).

People who have an adjustment disorder aren't weak or crazy. In fact, adjustment disorder is the most common type of emotional problem that psychiatrists diagnose in children and young adults. According to *The Harvard Medical Letter,* 42 percent of the young adults admitted to a psychiatric emergency room had an adjustment disorder. Changes in their lives have upset them so much that they need assistance to get back to normal. *The Harvard Medical Letter* also reported that 14 percent of suicides in people between 14 and 30 years old could be traced to an adjustment disorder.

Positive Ways to Get through Hard Times

Although teenagers' lives may not be falling apart from stress, all the changes can still get them down—even when they keep reminding themselves that the problems caused by their parents' divorce are only temporary. When circumstances around them are out of their control, they can take charge of some other things in their lives and make it easier for themselves.

Some people seem to have better ability to recover from a change or setback than others. Part of our capability to bounce back may have to do with the personality characteristics that we inherited from our parents and they inherited from theirs. Most coping skills, positive ways to get through hard times, can be learned. Learning healthy methods to cope with life's difficulties, including divorce, is something very much in our control.

If we're lucky, we can look to our family and friends to show us good ways of coping with stress. When we aren't so fortunate, we can broaden our circle of mentors by observing and talking with teachers or other trusted adults in our lives. We can even take a look at what life's survivors whom we don't know so well do in order to cope with the stress they experience when they face difficult times in their lives.

Some positive coping skills young people might want to try when the changes they are going through because of their parents' divorce seem overwhelming are

Sticking to old routines as much as possible. Visitation and maybe even moving can throw familiar habits into turmoil for a time, but teenagers can help themselves feel more secure in the middle of transition if they keep as much of their lives the same as before their parents' divorce. If you always go to bed by 10:30 on school nights and midnight on weekends, stick to that habit as best you can. If you always eat breakfast, then keep on eating it. Go to school, exercise, watch your regular television shows.

Establishing new routines. Sometimes when we're faced with too many new people and events in our lives, we get to the point of not knowing what to do first. If that happens, many of us tell ourselves we'll get our act together tomorrow and we don't do anything. One way to make new routines for ourselves and to start moving ahead in our lives is to make daily lists of the things we want and need to do. Even if we can't check off all the items at the end of the day, by making a list we establish a pattern for our activities and have some idea about what's going to happen next. People make daily lists because it helps them to feel secure and it gives them a sense of accomplishment.

Learning to start meeting our own needs. Take some time to think about ways you can make yourself feel better when you're under stress. Maybe you are the kind of person who needs quiet time so you can collect your thoughts. Or maybe the best thing you can do for yourself when you're feeling blue is to call a friend. Jeremy liked to escape to the dollar movies when things got too much for him. Selena made herself tapioca pudding, which made her feel better because her grandma used to make it for her when she was a little girl. Everyone needs to take their mind off their troubles temporarily, but it is important to remember that using alcohol or drugs to numb ourselves to our problems never works.

Learning to ask for what we need. Even in the best of times, parents are not mind readers. When they are caught up in dealing with their own emotional issues raised by divorce, they usually don't have the time or the energy to guess what it is we want or need. Your need to learn to tell them. If you're desperate to hear some kind of reassurance, ask for it. If you don't like being expected to take sides when your parents argue, let them know in a polite but firm way. When you tell people what you need from them, you won't always get it, but if you never ask, your chances of having your needs met are even lower.

Starting to look at life in a positive way. Even though divorce may make it seem like a young adult's family is falling apart, there are still some good parts to relationships with parents, grandparents, and brothers and sisters. Make a list of the positive things about your family. Those positive things are strengths; survivors know how to concentrate on them and use them to lean on in difficult times. They know how to make the most of what they have, instead of causing themselves to feel bad about what they can't have. This skill enables them to feel good about themselves no matter what is going on around them. They understand that change forces us to grow, and even though nobody really likes growing pains, they are part of life.

Learning to view ourselves in a positive way. Just as you came up with the positive qualities of your relationships with the people around you, think about the good things you have going for you—your skills, interests, and good qualities. Take some quiet time and make a list of what it is you like about yourself. Remember the times you surprised yourself by being calm in a crisis, or learned to do something you never imagined you could. When you acknowledge the things about yourself you are proud of, and your good qualities, you raise your self-esteem. By developing healthy self-esteem you begin to know and trust yourself. That knowledge and trust will carry you over the rough spots in life—including divorce.

Building a support network. While we need to learn to stand on our own emotional feet, we also must accept the fact that we need support from other people to help us through life's storms. Reaching out to friends and extended family members such as aunts and uncles and grandparents to start building relationships that aren't completely focused on our parent's divorce helps us to reclaim our own lives apart from our troubles. People who have some distance from the problems we are going through can often offer good advice and encouragement. They can help us get our minds going in other directions besides just thinking about what is bothering us.

Taking life one day at a time. People who survive stress well know that during times of turmoil they can't plan too far ahead, and they know that worrying about what might happen is just a waste of time. Neither do they dwell on the past, wishing things could go back to the way they were yesterday. When we live in the present and take the present one day, or even one minute, at a time, we make life easier for ourselves. Stress doesn't last forever. By staying in the moment, children of divorce can take their problem times in stride and begin working on solutions instead of being defeated by a choice they had little or no say in making.

3

Feeling and Dealing with Emotions

No matter how you look at it, divorce involves loss. Couples whose relationships end lose more than just the legal status of being married. They lose many of the daily patterns and interactions that they have established in their lives, including some that involve their children. Newly divorced adults may be happy to put some of these patterns, like the conflicts, behind them. The good parts of their marriage aren't so easy to let go of, but in order to heal and continue on with their lives, they must unhook from each other emotionally, giving up the plans they had as a couple. They need to surrender the happily-ever-after dream that they will spend the rest of their lives living with each other and their children in one household.

Children also lose many things during and after a divorce. Some of their losses are big and very obvious, like when Selena's father temporarily stopped seeing her. During the weeks he cut off contact with her, she felt abandoned because it seemed that he had totally turned his back on her. She went over and over the reasons he could have for not calling. Sometimes, she felt mad, but most of the time she was frightened that something she had done or maybe something about the kind of person she was had driven him away.

Others losses are more subtle. Jeremy missed being able to see his aunts and uncles on his mother's side as often as he wanted to because they pulled back during the divorce, unwilling to get drawn into his parents' battles. He also felt lonely for his friends from school during the time he spent at his father's house. He couldn't just walk down the block to see them.

Bobbi missed the family routine. Nearly every Sunday morning her father had cooked waffles and the whole family sat around the table reading the papers and talking about their week. When she and her brothers stayed with him, he still cooked, but the fact that her mother was missing from the table, and they gathered in a different kitchen, made her feel sad. Her dad took the family dog to live with him, so when she was at her mom's, she missed feeding it and playing with it, too.

Sometimes young adults whose parents divorce feel a sense of loss that is hard to pin down or put a name to because they've lost something that can't be seen or touched. If all their lives they grew up believing that their parents could do nothing wrong and suddenly the conflicts sparked by the marriage break-up make them see their mother and father in a new light, they have lost the childhood belief that their parents are perfect. Some young adults lose their faith in marriage. They decide that it isn't the good thing they've been told and promise themselves that they won't fall into the trap their parents did. When parents make promises they can't keep and break them, their children lose trust.

What people, activities, and beliefs do you think you might miss if your lifestyle changed because your family went through a divorce? If your parents have divorced, what do you feel lonely for?

Grief: Moving Through the Loss

The process of coming to terms with what we have lost is called *grief*. Although some believe that people go through the grieving process only when a loved one dies, that is far from the truth. To one extent or another, we must grieve for every loss in our lives—from failing a math test, and losing the belief that we are geniuses, to having a best friend die and not only losing the friendship but the idea that life goes on forever.

Mental health professionals who have studied the grieving process tell us that it is divided into several stages and that moving through those stages takes time. Elisabeth Kubler Ross, who worked with death and dying for many years, was the first mental health professional to divide the grieving process into a series of steps. The stages of grief are

- denial,
- anger,
- bargaining,
- sadness, and
- acceptance.

Using these steps to help people take a look at what they can expect to experience after a loss is helpful, but it is important to know that moving through the stages of grief isn't a neat progression. People can move forward for a while and then, all of a sudden, take a step back. At other times, a grieving person may experience feelings from two stages at once. Even though the journey through the grieving process has twists and turns, it is a journey forward to a time when the hurt feelings the loss has caused are healed.

Denial
When faced with a major loss in their lives, most people go into a state of emotional shock. The degree of shock they feel depends on the importance of what they have

lost. Shock causes people to shut down emotionally, and to pretend what is happening to them really isn't happening. This is called denial.

When Selena first learned that her father had left her mother, all she felt was a coldness in the pit of her stomach. For days she walked through her life feeling as numb as she imagined a zombie must be. It was as if something inside her had died. She didn't want to talk about her parents' separation or even think about it. Whenever she caught her mind turning to the question—what next?—she told herself that her father would walk through the door any minute, say it was all a big joke, and her life would get back to normal. When that didn't work, she'd plop herself down in front of the television set and sit there with her eyes and her mind glued to the screen.

Sometimes when people are in the denial stage, they minimize what is happening to them. They might not fully deny the loss, but they refuse to admit that they have any feelings about it. Jeremy actually made jokes about his parents' divorce to his friends. He even had himself and them convinced that it was no big deal to him. He told himself that what was happening in his household might affect his sister, but that he was almost a man and he could handle it and, besides, the divorce was better for everybody. Sure, it might cause some minor inconveniences, but what his parents decided and did had nothing to do with him.

Bobbi's denial had a different way of showing itself. She threw herself into helping around the house and taking charge of her younger brothers so that she had little time to feel anything. In the free time that remained she took up a whirlwind of activities, including joining a program to tutor elementary school students, and raising money for a church youth group trip. Everything she did was for some person or some cause outside of herself, and each activity took her further and further away from her feelings and thoughts about her own life. When her parents asked her how she was handling the divorce, she told them, "Fine," because she really thought she was doing fine.

People deny their emotions and the events around them in order to protect themselves from having to deal with the issues that loss raises in their lives. Temporary denial helps us to keep doing the things we need to do in the immediate crisis during the loss without being so overwhelmed by our feelings that we are helpless when action is required of us.

Although denial serves this purpose on a short-term basis, later on, ignoring our feelings and trying to go on as if nothing upsetting had occurred keeps us emotionally stuck in the crisis. Like a covered pot of water on a simmering stove, the steam of our emotions keeps building. Even though we may try to keep the lid of our denial tightly closed, our emotions build up pressure and escape when we least expect them to.

Anger

After their numbness starts wearing off, most people who have suffered loss expect to feel sad. They are surprised to feel anger instead. They are often mad at and betrayed by the person who hurt or left them and angry at the world for letting the loss happen. Sometimes they are furious at themselves for not stopping the loss from occurring and may spend time going over events in their mind trying to discover what they might have done to make things turn out differently.

Having a short temper is one sign that they are in the anger stage of the grieving process. Things that would normally irritate them just a little bit, like friends not calling when they say they will or the store being out of their favorite kind of soda, get them really mad. Other signs of anger are talking in a loud voice; fighting with parents, friends, or teachers; and talking back to authority figures.

Teenagers sometimes are especially angry at their mothers and fathers for getting a divorce, because they are already going through a time in their lives when they are critical of their parents. This judgmental phase is a normal and necessary part of getting ready to leave home and live independently. Add a difficult circumstance such as a divorce that brings out the worst side in any adult to the adolescent irritation already present, and a young adult's temper can flare in a major way.

When he finally stopped denying that his parents' divorce had affected him, Jeremy took turns blaming his mother and his father for all the disruption in his life their divorce had caused. Even though he didn't have to listen to their fighting all of the time now, he missed many things about the way his life had been. On some days, when he thought about it, his mother seemed like the villain because she always seemed to pick fights with his father. On other days, he felt like his father was in the wrong. What it all came down to was that they had acted, and continued to act, like a couple of bratty little kids, he thought. All they would have had to do was to talk with each other like adults and be willing to compromise sometimes. To Jeremy, it seemed like his parents had put their pride at always having to be right before his needs and the needs of his sister. They were stupid and selfish people, he thought.

Selena's anger was directed primarily at her father. When he called after his absence from her life, she felt as though she hated him. He had no right to leave and then come back as if nothing had happened. How could he have abandoned her? She wanted to cut him out of her life, never seeing him or thinking about him again. Even though she hung up on him, he kept calling. Her mother told her that because her dad had been granted visitation rights, she couldn't refuse to see him. The first time she visited him, Selena was so angry she couldn't even bring herself to talk to him.

Some teenagers aren't angry so much at their parents as they are at their situation, or life in general. Instead of being targeted at a specific person or persons, their anger becomes a grouchy attitude they carry toward the whole world. Life seems unfair to them. Why do they have to be the ones whose parents are seeing divorce lawyers?

Even though anger can be positive because it is part of the grieving process, and means a person is moving one step closer to healing from loss, feeling too much anger or expressing it inappropriately can cause trouble in young adults' lives. Bobbi had to spend a week in the school detention hall because she made a rude remark to her English teacher who criticized her for handing her home-work in late. Other young people, whose anger takes a physical form, can find themselves in even more hot water.

When anger gets out of hand, here are some things to try

- **Take time out.** Remove yourself from the situation or the person you are angry at by walking away and doing something else. You don't need to slam the door, just tell the person you are willing to talk later when you calm down, and then leave.
- **Get some physical exercise.** Walking, running, swimming, any physical activity causes your brain to release endorphins, neurotransmitters (brain chemicals) that act as natural tranquilizers. Not only will you improve your mood, but physical exercise will help keep your body healthy.
- **Find harmless ways to release your anger.** Sometimes people are so mad, they say and do things they later regret. If you think that is going to happen to you, write your feelings down in a journal or write a let-ter to the person you're angry with, then rip it up.
- **Talk your feelings out with someone who isn't directly involved in the conflict**. By speaking to friends, teachers, school counselors, and youth group leaders about the way you feel, you allow yourself to

work past the anger toward solutions for what is upsetting you.

- **When you feel ready to talk about your anger to the person you are angry with, do so without blaming or name-calling.** Instead, take responsibility for your feelings by saying, "*I feel* angry about . . . . ," not, "*You make* me angry when . . . ."

What are some effective ways that you have found to deal with your angry feelings?

Bargaining

Once anger starts decreasing, the bargaining stage of the grieving process begins. During this phase, our minds try to think of ways to undo the loss and put everything back the way it was before. Some people bargain with God, believing that if they do things in a certain way, then God will restore their loss.

More commonly, people bargain with themselves, convincing themselves that, if they are perfect, their loss will be reversed and everything will be the same as it was before the loss occurred. After Bobbi had to do detention, she started thinking that maybe her behavior was one of the reasons her parents broke up. It wasn't that she'd ever done anything terrible, but maybe just the typical teenage stuff she was going through had put a strain on their marriage. There had been times when she asked her father for money too often, and frequently she'd tried to slide out of doing the dishes or cleaning house when it was her turn. She'd started making sarcastic remarks to them, too, and her grades weren't what they could have been. Maybe if she tried harder to be a better person, they would at least think about getting back together and trying to make a happy family.

Many young adults, like Bobbi, whose parents are divorced, harbor a secret hope that they can get them back together again. Some young adults go further than she did, carrying stories back and forth and setting up situations so that they can manipulate their mother and father into remarrying. Although schemes like these sometimes work in the movies, in real life they often backfire.

Sadness

After a while, anger and bargaining can no longer keep our sorrow at bay. When we lose something, we miss it. The longing we feel when we know we can never get something back is not an easy feeling to live with. For a time, we may feel as though nothing could ever make us happy again.

After she got over being angry, Selena believed nothing could ever fill the empty space her dad had left when he moved out of the house. Even though her mother had packed all of her father's belongings and moved them to the garage, reminders of his presence still lingered. The blue ribbon from the science fair hanging on her wall was for a project he'd helped her on. The watch she wore to school every day was one he'd picked out for her last birthday. Whenever she looked at them she thought of his leaving and that he would probably never come back to stay. Those times she felt like crying. Sometimes, she did cry—so hard it seemed to her that she might never be able to stop.

Unhappiness is not a pleasant feeling. Living with the discomfort it causes us when we allow ourselves to experience it is painful, but it is necessary in order for us to heal from our losses. Sometimes our discomfort makes other people, especially those still in the denial stage of grief, uncomfortable as well. They may have a hard time observing our sadness and hearing us express it because of what they are feeling. Parents who have an exceptionally difficult time with their children's sadness after a divorce are often denying the sadness they feel at their own loss. They are afraid to feel their own abandonment, hurt, and unhappiness, so they try to avoid anything that might trigger those feelings.

Selena's mother kept telling her to cheer up and, when that didn't work, she bought her candy and ice cream as though she were a little girl and a bag of licorice twists would make the hurt go away. Jeremy's dad told him to act like a man when he was feeling down. He said that it was weak to show his emotional pain or even to feel it, that real men didn't let things like a divorce bother them. Bobbi's mom and dad encouraged her to talk about her feelings, but when she shared her unhappiness about the divorce with them, she could tell they didn't really want to hear it. Neither one of them could look at her and they kept trying to change the subject.

Divorcing parents sometimes have trouble accepting the sadness their children feel because they feel guilty. Even though they believe that the divorce is the best thing for themselves and their children in the long run, they feel bad about the hurt their children feel because of their decision. Other parents who are angry get even angrier when they know that their children miss their former spouse. Instead of allowing them to feel and express their emotions, they tell their children that the other parent is in the wrong, and they try to get their children to feel anger instead of loss.

No matter how painful loss is, feeling sad is better than the alternative. People who don't let themselves get to this stage of the grieving process can remain stuck in anger or bargaining, sometimes for years. They may be able to get by in their lives, but they do not heal. So much of their time and energy is spent hiding out from their emotional pain, they have little left for anything except maintaining their denial.

Sadness makes us temporarily feel as if there is no hope for the future. We look at the world, not through rose-colored glasses, but through dark ones that seem to put a dark cast on everything we see. During this time, it may seem that the blues will go on forever. In most cases they don't. Once we've truly allowed ourselves to feel our loss, we can let it go.

Slowly the times that we feel in low spirits become further and further apart and the unhappiness doesn't last so long. Most of us start to pay attention to the good things around us and get interested in life once again. There's too much we want to do with our time to spend it feeling sorry for ourselves because something important to us is missing.

Some young people get stuck in the sadness phase of grieving. When that happens it is called depression. For months the unhappiness lingers to the point that depressed people stop caring about life. No matter what they try, nothing works—they just can't seem to snap out of it. Depressed people can't get motivated to do much of anything, and they don't feel pleasure from the activities in life that would normally make them happy. They just don't care about anything anymore. Some of them don't want to live and even think of ways of ending their lives.

Depression is a a serious illness. It is the most common emotional problem people face—one in four women and one in 10 men will experience it at some point in their lifetime. Depression can have a happy ending. Professional mental health workers can treat the problem with psychotherapy or medication. If you or someone you know had felt sad and maybe hopeless, helpless, and irritable for a period of time, a visit to a counselor, psychologist, or psychiatrist may be in order.

When a person experiences four or more of the symptoms listed below for two weeks or longer, they need to seek professional help.

- a change in sleeping habits, sleeping more or less than usual, getting up early in the morning, sleeping too much or not being able to go to sleep at night;
- forgetfulness and lack of concentration;
- feelings of hopelessness that just won't go away;
- feelings of worthlessness;
- lack of joy and laughter in life, and a loss of interest in activities that used to be enjoyable;

- appetite changes, either eating less or more than usual;
- tiredness;
- feelings of guilt;
- irritability and restlessness;
- thoughts of suicide.

Acceptance

The final stage of the grieving process is called acceptance. A young adult who has moved into the acceptance phase hasn't forgotten the losses the divorce has caused, and probably still misses what is no longer a part of his or her life. Acceptance means that the grieving person no longer uses anger, bargaining, or sorrow to get back what is gone or has forever changed. Instead that person has been able to let go of the loss and move on to new things in life. Acceptance is a sign of healing.

Jeremy, who really missed being able to go out into the yard and shoot hoops with his father every night after dinner, and who secretly feared that his dad was pulling away from him emotionally after moving out of the house, eventually started feeling better about their relationship. Even though his dad wasn't there to play basketball in the evenings, he maintained contact by calling his father between weekend visits. His dad bought a membership in a health club and one night a week Jeremy met him there to work out. Although the things he did with his dad were different than before, Jeremy still liked their time together. He especially liked the sauna at the club.

The time of moving from our old, familiar lifestyles toward the new is one of uncertainty. Sometimes when we lose something, whether it is time spent with a parent, or an old routine, our lives seem empty while we wait for other things to fill the space left by our loss. During that period we may feel like we are stuck, and that nothing is happening, or that we will never feel better—especially if the people around us seem impatient with us.

Sometimes our own impatience may drive us to try and fill the emptiness with too much television, food, activity, or even alcohol or drugs. Those things temporarily fill us, but soon we feel empty again and need more of whatever we were using in order to feel good about ourselves. In the meantime, we avoid feeling the emotions associated with the loss that has come to us from the divorce. In the end we may develop an addiction and wind up with more problems to solve than we had in the first place. And when we've solved those, we're still faced with moving through the grieving process.

Even though it may seem as though we aren't going forward with our lives when we grieve, we are making progress. Sometimes, because so much the work of grieving happens inside of us, it isn't noticeable to others. As we move through the grief process, we stop looking over our shoulders and trying to grasp what we can no longer have. By the time we reach the acceptance stage, we are looking ahead and have freed ourselves to embrace the new opportunities life brings our way.

Dealing with Feelings

Besides the anger and sadness that are stages in grieving for our losses, young people whose parents are divorcing often experience a number of other emotions. Some of the feelings that can follow divorce are guilt, shame, confusion, worry, anger, jealousy, fear, loneliness, and rejection.

Guilt

Occasionally teenagers tell themselves that they are the main reason their parents are divorcing. When they see signs that Mom or Dad are feeling sadness or anger, a natural part of what they have to go through to finish *their* grieving, they blame themselves for that, too. Because they are certain that their parents' negative feelings are all their fault, they may keep on trying to "fix" their parents long after they've given up on fixing their parents' broken marriage.

If you

- feel like you are walking on eggshells, having to be very careful not to make anybody feel upset;
- put pressure on yourself to help your parents solve their problems; and
- try to guess the response your parents want or need from you and provide it before they ask,

chances are, you are feeling guilty.

Teenagers in the middle of a guilt trip need to remind themselves that they are not the cause of their parents' divorce, even if they are one of the topics parents argue over. The divorce is caused by conflicts between parents, not between parents and children. Young adults cannot reverse what is happening. Just as they cannot change the situation, they can't keep their parents from feeling uncomfortable feelings about the divorce, no matter how hard they try.

Shame

While guilt comes from thinking you did something bad or wrong, shame is the feeling you have when you believe you, yourself, are bad or wrong. Children and young adults learn to feel shame when they are told they are no good. We also learn to feel shame when our emotional bond with someone we love and depend on is broken. Usually we interpret that loss of connectedness as rejection, meaning we are no longer lovable.

At the center of divorce is a broken emotional tie between two adults. One or both parents may be feeling some shame and rejection from what they are going through. Out of anger, they may say or do things that they feel ashamed about later. Often those feelings are intensified when friends and even family members avoid people who are getting a divorce because the situation triggers their emotional discomfort. Sometimes people who are getting a divorce are given the cold shoulder, or actually condemned, by people who do not believe in divorce.

Young people can catch shameful feelings from their parents much as they can catch a cold or the flu. When parents act as though they are ashamed of themselves, and they cannot bring themselves to talk about their feelings, it affects the whole family. Without ever being fully aware of what it is they have to be ashamed about, children start to feel there is something drastically wrong or flawed about their family, and that they are not as good as other people. Parents may also avoid dealing with their own shame by telling their children that they ought to be ashamed of themselves for their feelings.

Even though, in most instances, divorcing parents do not completely cut their ties with their children, getting to spend less time with a parent may cause young adults to feel abandoned. Having a mother or father move out of the house when you've always lived with him or her isn't a pleasant thing to endure. When it happens, it is hard to believe that you didn't play a part in your parent's leaving.

In order to stop the negative effects of shame on our lives, we first need to recognize that shame is what we are feeling. If you

- feel worthless,
- believe one you don't deserve love, or
- blame yourself for things you have no control over,

you are probably feeling shame.

The tricky thing about shame is that when we feel it, we are usually ashamed to talk about it. Sometimes we're even ashamed about feeling ashamed. We don't want to admit our shame to other people because they might say or do something to confirm our belief that we aren't worthy of love and that something is so wrong with us that we will never be able to fix it.

We also may keep from admitting to ourselves that we're feeling ashamed. One way of doing this is to become perfectionistic, trying never to make mistakes. Or we may isolate ourselves from people, or we may procrastinate, putting off the things we need to do out of fear that we'll do them wrong and people will find out how bad or incompetent we are.

When we try to keep our shameful feelings secret from others or from ourselves, they get bigger and bigger until they take over our lives. By isolating ourselves so that no one will discover the awful truth about us, we soon believe that we are unique and that nobody else has feelings like ours. In order to work through our shame, we need to talk it out with other people. Support groups, friends, parents, counselors can listen to what we have to say. Just the fact that our feelings of unworthiness are no longer secret is enough to start putting them in their place. When we find out that other people feel the same way we do, our shame begins to disappear.

Worry and Fear

When parents divorce, many of the things that young adults took for granted in their daily lives suddenly vanish—so does their sense of security. No longer can they predict what will happen next month, or even tomorrow, because so many things are out of young people's control. The less information people have about the changes taking place in their lives, the more they tend to worry about what will happen next.

Even when we're well informed about what is happening, we still can feel insecure because we have no control over what is going on in our families. We may be able to make better educated guesses, but we still can't predict for sure what will happen to our families or to us next. There's no way to stop the divorce or to put our families back together again, no matter how much we want things to go back to the way they were. About all we can do is to take care of ourselves and hope for the best. Since most young adults have never experienced divorce, they usually have little way of knowing what the best for themselves and their families should be in that situation.

Some young adults whose parents are divorcing worry about money. They wonder if there will be enough to pay the rent and put food on the table. They get upset by not knowing for sure if the parent who moved out will stick around or eventually move even further away—like out of state. They may be anxious about the possibility of having to move and change schools. They might fear that no marriage could ever work and that they will never find a lasting relationship with someone they love when they are older.

Even though they may not express it, young people often worry about their parents. They think about what the future would hold if something happened to their custodial parent and there was no one to take care of them. When parents are extremely angry at one another, their children might fear they will become violent. If a parent seems to be depressed over the divorce, teenagers often become afraid that Mom or Dad will become suicidal. The anxiety escalates when they see their parents reacting to the divorce by drinking too much or showing other self-destructive behaviors.

As we discussed in the last chapter, any kind of change can cause people to feel nervous because it temporarily takes away the sense of security. Some of the signs that you are worrying too much are

- not wanting to let a parent out of your sight,
- being overprotective with parents or brothers and sisters,
- feeling jumpy or restless for no clear reason,
- having a hard time sleeping, or
- having a hard time concentrating on anything but the divorce and trying to figure out what might happen next.

Sometimes the anxiety young people feel, especially during and right after a divorce, gradually goes away by itself once life starts smoothing out. As what will happen next in a young person's world becomes easier to predict, calmness and peace of mind return. Even so, during the time that we are worried, anxiety can make our lives more difficult than they need to be.

After life has settled into new patterns and becomes familiar and secure once again, some young people still worry. Anxiety has become a habit and when the old reasons for feeling stressed out go away, they find new things that upset them. People who feel anxious for long periods of time often develop physical problems from their over-reaction to stress. Because nervousness keeps the body's immune system from working at its top levels, they may catch more colds than usual. Headaches, muscle aches, and stomachaches can also be caused by too much worry.

Although doctors can provide tranquilizers and other antianxiety medications to calm people down, there are other things we can do to stop ourselves from worrying so much. One of the most effective is to learn to slow down and live in the present, finding good things to enjoy in each moment as it comes. We can't undo the past, and, unless we have psychic powers, we can't tell what the future will hold, so why worry about it? Most of the things we fear never come to pass anyway.

Other worry-stopping strategies that work are exercise, a healthful diet, and relaxation techniques. One of the best non-prescription tranquilizers is your imagination. Take some quiet time to picture in your mind a place where you felt calm. It might be the seashore with the waves pounding against the sand or a woods with tall green trees and birds singing. Next time you start feeling unsettled, breathe deeply and slowly and go there in your mind. Many stores sell relaxation tapes with nature sounds that help you in your imaginary journey. Other tapes have guided imagery scripts that lead listeners to imagine peaceful scenes and events.

When tension makes us tighten our muscles, we can relax them by slowly tensing and relaxing all the way from our toes to our head, one part of our bodies at a time. Put this book down for a minute and check out how it feels. Starting with your toes, curl them up tightly and hold them that way while you count slowly to five. Then relax them and count to five again. Next tighten the muscles in the calves of your legs and relax them, now try your thighs, then your stomach and then your shoulder muscles, your hands and your arms. Now notice how you feel. If you are like most people, your muscles will have let go of some of the tension they carried. Try this exercise again before you go to sleep and see what happens.

Confusion

Confusion—scrambled thinking and mixed emotions—is a state that often goes hand in hand with worry and fear. It is the mind's response to uncertainty. When people are confused, they can't seem to focus on or to make up their minds about anything. Young adults whose parents are divorcing get emotionally confused when their mothers and fathers don't or can't let them know what is happening, or when they push them into taking sides in the adult conflicts, choosing one parent over the other. For some teenagers, confusion is limited to issues having to do with their parents' divorce. Others find these mixed-up feelings seeping over into other areas of their lives.

Chaotic thoughts and feelings are a normal part of being a young person. One of the jobs of maturing into adulthood is trying out a number of emotions, attitudes, and activities. Because teenagers are in transition from being children to becoming grownups, they are often very logical and mature one moment, then turn around and do or say something a child would. They decide to hang out with one group of friends and then exchange them for another. One month a teenager might want to go to medical school to become a doctor, and the next to operate heavy equipment at a construction site. Add the confusion divorce can bring to the back and forth swings all teenagers experience, and the result can be feeling like a crazy, mixed-up kid.

Confused people often find they are able to do less and less because doing things first requires choosing what to do, and then deciding which part of it to do. When our thoughts are scrambled by confusion, we don't know what we want or where to begin. Or once we begin, we change our minds, do something else, change our minds again, start something else, and rarely get anything finished.

Inner turmoil makes it almost impossible for people to focus enough to study, do their homework, clean their rooms, or sometimes even hold an intelligent conversation. They simply aren't able to organize their thoughts well enough to do so.

If parents aren't aware that their actions can create inner conflicts for teenagers when they push or manipulate them into taking sides in a divorce, emotional chaos can rule. Young people in this situation often feel torn in half, almost as though they have split personalities. They decide their mother is to blame for the divorce and then two minutes later, they feel differently—it's Dad who is the villain. Feeling this way is called having a *loyalty conflict*. When you are feeling loyalty conflicts, you don't know whom to trust or believe, so you wind up not trusting or believing anyone.

The signs of feeling confused by uncertainty or loyalty conflicts are

- procrastination, or delaying getting things done,
- changing your mind several times before you can make a decision,
- feeling torn or wrong after you've made one, or
- idealizing one parent and putting down another.

Reacting to major life changes with confusion is normal. Most of the time, our confusion starts to clear up when we know the facts about what is happening to us and don't feel pressured to take sides. We can deal with confusion by asking questions in order to get the information we need about what is happening in our lives, and by keeping ourselves out of the middle of conflicts between other people. We'll discuss more about how to avoid taking sides during divorce later in this book.

Hurt

When our feelings are hurt, we feel like we have been injured by another's words or actions. Somehow it seems as though what they have done or said not only has the power to inflict pain on us, but that it diminishes our sense of who we are. Having hurt feelings once in a while is a normal part of living and loving other people. When we care about people, we care about what they think of us and we make ourselves vulnerable to them. If they unfairly criticize us or attack us out of anger, our feelings are hurt. If they make promises to us and break them, or they avoid us, we interpret their actions to mean that they don't love us, and we feel injured.

When young adults experience divorce in the family, they are bound to experience some insecurity about who they are and how they fit into their family, because the family is taking a different shape. They may question where they belong and just how much their parents love them. If their parents are caught up in their own emotional struggles to come to terms with the divorce, they may unknowingly say or do things that cause their children to have hurt feelings. Even off-handed comments—such as "You're just like your father; you never listen to me," or, "You're always asking me for money, just like your mother does"—can sting like a slap across the face.

When we can't let remarks like these go, and have trouble stopping thinking about our hurts, carrying them around and letting our thoughts dwell on them, hurt feelings becomes a pattern in our lives. The more we nurse our wounds, the more we make ourselves vulnerable to further hurt. Our self-esteem becomes more and more dependent on what other people do and think about us rather than what we're doing and how we think about ourselves. Over time it seems as if we grow antennae that can detect negativity directed toward us even when people don't do or say hurtful things. We tell ourselves that they are thinking bad thoughts about us, that they don't like us, and that they don't want anything to do with us— and we start seeing ourselves as victims.

Some ways to tell if hurt feelings have become a pattern in your life are noticing whether or not you are

- taking negative comments and criticism personally even though they aren't directed at you,
- feeling like a victim that other people are out to get,
- hearing many people tell you that you are too sensitive or that you are overreacting,
- forgetting the good things people say about you and the nice things they do by telling yourselves the other person didn't mean it, or
- feeling resentful and angry for being used by other people.

When teenagers grow up in a family where they have experienced verbal or physical abuse, or where one or both parents was dependent on alcohol or drugs, they are especially familiar with hurt feelings. Chances are they have taken in, or *internalized,* the criticisms of others and made them part of the inner picture of themselves that they constantly carry around. They become dependent on other people to define who they are and how they feel. The more tarnished that picture becomes, the more they learn to look outside themselves for self-esteem or a sense of self-worth.

As that happens their emotional boundaries weaken. They have a difficult time telling where they leave off and where other people begin. They let other people get to them because they confuse the feelings of others with their own. Instead of shrugging their shoulders and walking away for a little while to get a sense of perspective back, they try to move even closer, doing everything in their power to please that person. When they finally do try to get some distance, they go too far in the other direction, cutting themselves off from a person or people in order to protect themselves.

One of the best ways to take care of our hurt feelings is to learn to unhook or detach from our dependence on others to make us feel good about ourselves. Sometimes people do or say hurtful things because *they* are hurting, and often their emotional pain comes from a reason that has nothing to do with us. Once we stop blaming ourselves for how other people feel, we can stop beating ourselves up over situations and events over which we have no control or for which we have no responsibility.

When we learn ways to make ourselves feel good, even though other people ignore us or put us down, we get over our hurt feelings quickly. One way to do this is to compliment ourselves and turn our minds to the things we like about who we are. Take a few minutes to make a list of your good qualities and the accomplishments you are proud of. They might range from learning to ride a bike when you were younger to being able to make your grandpa, who lives in a nursing home, laugh. If you have trouble thinking of items to write down, don't worry, they will come to your mind. Leave the list where you can see it and when you think of something, write it down.

When you finish, start another list of things you can do to make yourself feel good—activities that aren't dependent on other people. Some examples might be reading a horror novel or watching an action-packed video. Things like taking a walk in the woods or working out might go on your list, too. Because you are a unique person, the things you write on your list will be different from those another person might jot down. That's okay.

Next time your feelings are hurt, pull out your lists and review the things about yourself you feel proud of, then do something that will help you to feel better. Once this becomes a habit, you won't need to use your lists anymore, because you will automatically know when you need nurturing and what to do to take care of yourself.

Jealousy

One of the consequences of not being able to nurture ourselves and give ourselves love is that we get angry when other people don't provide us with the attention or affection that we want or need. We become jealous when we see them paying attention to other people, or their focus is turned toward activities that don't include us.

Even in the best of times, dependence on others to meet all of our emotional needs can give us a rough time, because we never seem to get enough of whatever it is we want from others. Getting what we want exactly when we want it from other people is almost impossible. During a divorce, looking to others to provide us with the self-esteem we lack has even a smaller chance of meeting with success.

Parents are busy making appointments with lawyers and trying to adjust to the major changes in their daily lives at the same time they are working through their own emotional issues. They don't always have the time to focus on their children or the children's needs. When they do, they may give more attention to the younger children and expect the young adults in the family to delay getting their needs met. It is no wonder that some teenagers begin to resent the time and attention their younger brothers and sisters get from their parents, and they start to feel jealous of them.

If a parent starts a new romantic relationship, that can trigger even more jealousy in teenagers. The new boyfriend or girlfriend is one more thing standing between the young person and what he or she wants—undivided attention from a parent. When Mom or Dad's new partner has children, there's even more room for jealousy.

You know that you are feeling jealousy when you find yourself

• comparing the new person Mom or Dad is dating to your biological mother or father,
• being competitive,

- clinging to people and being demanding,
- feeling a need to interrupt conversations.

Wanting more attention and reassurance than usual during a stressful time in life when you aren't feeling secure about the future is normal. Wanting another person's total attention all of the time is unreasonable. When you aren't paying attention to yourself, no amount of attention from others will make you feel better except for the moment or two in which it is given.

Jealousy usually backfires because when we feel it, we act in ways that drive people away from us rather than encouraging them to turn their attention to us. We might drive people away by being so possessive that we smother them or make them feel as though they are our hostages. We could be so demanding of their time and attention, or try to control their behavior so much, that they can't stand to be around us. We may try to manipulate them into paying attention to us by making them feel guilty if they don't give us what we want. Simmering resentments and full-blown anger about the way we try to make them feel, may be all the attention they want to give us.

One way we can learn to decrease our jealousy is to widen the circle of people around us. If a parent is too busy to spend time with you, chances are a good friend would like nothing more than to talk with you. If he or she is busy, probably another friend is available. Learning not to depend on only one or two people to meet our emotional needs helps increase our chances of getting what we want.

Jealousy grows fastest in people with low self-esteem. When we learn to boost our feelings of self-worth, our jealousy shrivels and dies. Positive self-talk and doing things to nurture ourselves, the same ways we learned to cope with hurt feelings, can help. When we learn to like ourselves, we aren't miserable if other people are busy and no one pays attention to us at the moment. Sometimes life provides us with time to be alone. We have a choice to enjoy those times and use them as opportunities to get in touch with ourselves, or we can choose to spend that time feeling jealous and lonely.

We have no say in the emotions we feel during times of turmoil in our lives. We can't run away from our grief or any of the difficult emotions that are part of life when parents divorce. How we deal with our emotions, all the emotions we've talked about—from anger, sadness, shame, and guilt to anxiety, confusion, hurt, and jealousy—is a choice we do have. If we want, we can deny our feelings and hide them deep inside where they will make us suffer, or we can let ourselves feel what we're feeling, deal with it in a constructive way, and allow the feeling to go, so there is room for new and positive feelings to come in. Choosing the latter course of action is taking the pathway toward healing.

4

Meeting the Challenges

During and after their parents' divorce, young adults confront a set of challenges that adolescents growing up in intact families never have to face. Although many young people feel temporarily overwhelmed by the emotions we discussed in the last chapter, they do not have to allow uncomfortable feelings or the changes in their lives to defeat them. The challenges are an opportunity to grow. Finding workable solutions for problems, and learning how to take care of oneself in spite of what is happening, can help young adults whose parents are divorcing to become capable, confident people in other areas of their lives.

The problems that nearly every child of divorce must face become more difficult to solve than they need to be when teenagers let their parents' divorce take up all of their time and energy. Sometimes it may seem as though every thought that comes into their minds has something to do with the break-up of their parents' marriage and what is happening to their family. They need to remember that, although they are affected by it, the divorce is something that is occurring between their parents. It is only part of their lives and—even though at the beginning it may be a big part—they need to learn to detach from their parents' problems and to focus on how the divorce is affecting them, and the things they can do to help make their own lives easier.

Some of the specific ways that teenagers can make the best of a tough situation and even find positives in the midst of the challenges that face them, include

- spending extra time with extended family members like grandparents, aunts, and uncles,
- getting involved in extracurricular activities at school,
- expressing feelings to family members,
- maintaining a circle of friends,
- talking with a trusted adult,
- spending time with each parent,
- trying to keeping daily routines as much as possible, and
- establishing new single-parent family traditions.

What Doesn't Work

Some teenagers believe they are tough enough to handle anything. They don't like to appear weak, either to themselves or to other people. They believe that showing feelings is a weakness. What they don't know is that people who don't acknowledge to themselves and to others what they are feeling—whether those emotions are sadness, anger, jealousy or anxiety—rarely think straight. Although they are just as smart as anybody else, because they haven't dealt with their feelings, especially feelings they are afraid to admit having, their emotions scream out for attention, and overpower their ability to reason and solve problems.

If they acknowledged their anger at the parent who moved out of the house, and talked to Mom or Dad about how they felt, chances are they would be able to think clearly once more and be able to brainstorm some ideas to help deal with the abandonment issues beneath the anger. Perhaps they could arrange to spend more time with their non-custodial parent, or they might decide to pick up the phone and give that parent a call rather than waiting for them to call, getting more fearful and angrier by the second when the phone doesn't ring.

The very human tendency of pushing uncomfortable feelings deep inside of us and trying to ignore them in the hope they will go away is why it is often easy for us to come up with good suggestions for friends about how to take care of what is wrong in their lives yet difficult to find solutions for our own struggles. Because we usually aren't caught up in the emotional whirlwind of other people's problems, we are able to gain a more objective perspective and easily see what they can do to help themselves out of their dilemmas. Sometimes we use that ability to offer good advice to others and to meet their emotional needs as a way of ignoring taking care of ourselves.

The unhealthy process of denying our feelings hurts us, and it can lead us to hurt others. When we ignore feelings, we develop what mental health professionals call *defense mechanisms,* ways of walling off our emotions so we don't have to feel them, and walling ourselves off from the world in the hope that we won't be hurt. Defense mechanisms are not only an attempt to protect ourselves from the hurtful feelings we are experiencing now, but also our way of protecting ourselves from any hurt we might possibly feel in the future.

Defense mechanisms are an unhealthy way young adults use to cope with painful situations like being caught in the middle of a custody battle, or knowing that a parent is unwilling to pay child support to help meet their basic needs for food and shelter. Unfortunately, the same defense mechanisms we use to block the emotionally painful experiences we have from our awareness, not only hold us back from our healing, but also serve as a barricade against the good things waiting to enter our lives. Even though they may seem to work in the short run, defense mechanisms keep us from facing and overcoming our challenges. When they become ineffective, we're still left with the same problems that caused us to put up the barriers in the first place.

Some of the common defense mechanisms teenagers use when their parents are divorcing follow.

Acting Out

When Bobbi's parents broke up, even though she felt like crying, she covered her hurt feelings with anger because she thought feeling abandonment and betrayal were babyish. She tried to hide the fact that she was mad about the divorce and at both of them, but her anger kept building. It had to come out some way, and it did. Her temper with friends was short, and it seemed like she wanted to argue over every little thing. Some days she felt like a porcupine with its quills sticking out so people wouldn't get too close. It was that way with her teachers, too, especially two of them who had never been her favorites. Now she talked back to them in a rude tone of voice when they asked her to do something, and she went on strike over her homework. As a result, her grades dropped.

In addition to being irritable, lying, fighting, and shoplifting or other forms of stealing are some ways teenagers act out the anger that they are unable to express in words. Rebelling is another way. A young adult may, out of anger at a parent that is triggered by the divorce, vow to be just the opposite of that parent and try to live that way. Some teenagers make new friends who act tough, and start using alcohol or drugs as an act of rebellion. Jeremy's sister started a sexual relationship with a young man she didn't really like. She was so angry sometimes she thought it would be a good thing if she got pregnant because it would teach her parents a lesson.

When we don't acknowledge our anger or talk about it, it becomes *free-floating*. No longer hooked to the person or situation that triggered it, it hovers around us like a huge dark cloud, sticking to other people and situations that get in our way. Sometimes free-floating anger causes us to rage at people who have done nothing to deserve our harsh words or angry actions. Just the fact that they are present in our lives is enough to make them the target of our tempers, like Bobbi's teachers were. People with free-floating anger are usually seen by others as being moody, irritable, or short-tempered. Sometimes they're said to have an attitude problem.

Usually, as in Bobbi's case, their anger and the acting out it causes cover hurt feelings that are very frightening to confront, because admitting that we feel them makes us feel weak and vulnerable. Acting out by being tough is a way to push other people away, including family members. If we don't allow them to get close to us and we drive them away with our actions, they can't hurt our feelings any more than we've been hurt already. Many teenagers who act out are operating from the position of "I'll get you before you get me."

Other times, acting out can be a way to get attention or a cry for help. Bobbi didn't want to feel the way she did and secretly she hoped that somebody would stop her from messing up in school and blowing apart her friendships. She didn't know how to ask for help, and the people she was closest to—her family members—seemed too busy to notice what was happening with her. Finally, in a family counselling session, the therapist confronted her silence and the stormy expression on her face. At first she denied that anything was wrong, but then the words came pouring out and she began crying after a few minutes. Afterward she felt better. It was as if an enormous pressure that had been building up inside of her had finally been released. After a few more times of talking about the feelings she had tried so desperately to hide, she didn't feel so grouchy anymore.

Being Controlling

Another defense mechanism that young adults may develop when their parents divorce is that of trying to control what goes on in their lives so that they will feel safe. Teenagers who feel that life is unpredictable and completely beyond their control because of the divorce might start making lists that detail how to spend every minute of their time throughout the day, and get upset when something happens to threaten their schedule— even a pleasant surprise like an invitation to go out for a hamburger or a movie.

For several months Selena tried to structure everything in her life so she could feel secure and avoid wondering what was going to happen next. What she couldn't structure, she tried to avoid, including TV shows about single-parent families, so she wouldn't have to think about anything that made her feel uncomfortable. She even started avoiding her best friend who might bring up her parents' divorce in conversation—something she didn't want to talk about. Soon she was isolating herself from people, including her parents, spending most of her time in her room to avoid life because she couldn't possibly call all the shots.

Another way people separate themselves from the temporarily unpredictable world caused by divorce, and insulate themselves against hurt feelings, is numbing out with alcohol and drugs. Overdoing activities that would normally be good for us, like exercise or studying, can also become a way to isolate and insulate ourselves, so that we have the illusion circumstances are within our control. Some young people, especially young women, develop the eating disorder anorexia, controlling their intake of food to the point of near-starvation in order to keep a tight rein over something that is a central part of their lives.

Often our control issues center on our relationships with other people, especially people who are part of our families. Common ways that we may use to try to control others in order to give the illusion that our lives are secure include

- being bossy,
- threatening to do something others won't like such as running away from home if we don't get our way,
- scolding people when they don't act the way we want them to,
- helping people when they don't want or need our assistance and see it as interference, and
- manipulating them into doing what we want them to do without ever coming out and directly asking for what it is we need from them.

When he was growing up in a family where both parents bickered nearly constantly, Jeremy had learned to play his parents against each other in order to get the answers from them that he wanted. It came as no surprise when he took advantage of their low energy and high stress levels during their divorce to escalate the tactic. When he wanted to do something like spend the night at a friend's, he carried what one parent had said privately to him to the other parent to get them fighting even more than usual. Once their attention was off him, he went ahead and did what he wanted. If his mother refused to give him an advance on his allowance, he would go to his father for the money, certain that if he played his cards right he would get what he wanted.

Becoming Victims

Some people who experience difficult times in their lives, like their parents' divorce, react to it by becoming victims. Instead of trying to take charge of everything and everyone around them, they are passive, allowing themselves to be controlled by others. Even though they feel sorry for themselves, and often manage to get others to feel the same way, becoming a victim is as much a defense mechanism as is bossing other people around, or acting out anger through rebellion.

Because of all the negative talk about broken homes and single-parent families, it is especially easy for some teenagers whose parents are getting divorced to think of themselves as helpless victims of the circumstances around them. When we lose things that are important to us, whether they be contact with a parent, the space we are used to living in, or our free time on Saturday mornings, one of our first tendencies is to feel sorry for ourselves. Before we know it we may be feeling helpless as well.

Sometimes Selena fell into the trap of self-pity. If she complained enough about her life since her parents' divorce, her grandparents would give her sympathy and talk to her mother to make her feel guilty, so she would angrily give in to her daughter's reluctance to help around the house. When Selena tearfully told her teachers that she couldn't do her homework because things were so bad at home, some of them excused her from doing it. The more Selena complained, the worse her problems seemed and the more helpless she felt. Soon her friends started avoiding her because all she wanted to talk about was how horrible her life was.

Playing the victim role may not appear at first glance to be a good defense mechanism. How can people who seem to think of nothing but their hurt feelings, and who sometimes deliberately put themselves in a position to be hurt and abused, be protecting themselves? While it is true that victims' feelings are constantly being injured, walking through life with a "poor me" attitude allows them to give up responsibility for themselves and find ways to get others to take care of them as it did for Selena. At the same time, they are able to blame someone else for everything that goes wrong in their lives. This allows them to maintain the illusion of control over their circumstances. No matter what happens to them, it isn't their fault. Because they are always able to point a finger at some "bad guy," they never have to look at the part they play in their problems.

Selena didn't have to look at how her attitude affected her relationship with her mother as long as she had her grandparents to serve as an audience to her complaints. Because she could convince them and her teachers to rescue her, she didn't have to take any responsibility for sometimes provoking her mother's anger, and for not doing her homework. After her mom heard the exaggerated stories she'd told her grandparents about having to be alone so much and do so many chores, she got really mad, but all that did was cause Selena to feel sorrier for herself and give her another excuse not to take charge of her life.

When we play the victim role, we confuse being taken care of with being cared for. Victims, often without being fully aware of what they are doing, take the position that philosophers call the "high moral ground." Because they view the people around them as bearing the blame for all their troubles, victims convince themselves that they are somehow better than those they are certain are victimizing them. People who convince themselves that no one understands or appreciates them and that they are being used by other people walk around with resentments at other people for not being able to read their minds and take care of them the way they want.

Changing Ourselves/Changing Our Lives

Even though they may become familiar habits, acting out our anger rather than talking it out, trying to control every little detail of our lives, or feeling helpless and defeated, don't work in the long run because they prevent us from examining and solving our problems. Dropping defense mechanisms means taking a risk and learning to look at and relate to the world and the people in it in a new way, one that may not feel very safe at first.

Taking risks can be very difficult, especially at times in our lives when our self-esteem is at an all-time low— which it tends to be when we're under stress, because we feel as though our families are coming apart at the seams. In order to gain the courage to drop our defense mechanisms, we must learn to feel good about ourselves. Only when we are committed to feeling our feelings and doing something about them instead of hiding behind defense mechanisms, can we begin to solve some of the problems facing us in our lives.

One of the most effective things anyone can do to make fundamental changes in herself or himself is to reach out to other people who can support them in their personal growth. Sometimes friends and relatives are able to provide us with the encouragement and guidance we need, but not always. Two places where we can get this kind of help are with mental health professionals, and in support groups.

Counselors, therapists, psychologists, social workers, and psychiatrists have received education and training so that they are familiar with the challenges faced by children of divorce. Although support groups may not be led by a professionally trained leader, their members share the same goal—to work through their problems and improve their lives. Because some group members have already found ways to solve many of the problems newcomers face, they can offer encouragement and practical suggestions. Sources for support groups and mental health professionals are listed at the end of this book.

Because helping professionals and support group members can't be with them every minute of the day, young adults need to learn some problem-solving skills in order to meet the challenges that sometimes occur on a daily basis in homes where parents have recently divorced. When young people learn to think about answers to the specific problems divorce may have put in their path, and to try solutions for those challenges, they need to remember that we can try to change other people, but too often our attempts are bossy or manipulative. When we try to make those around us feel guilty about what they are doing or order them to stop, they may try to change. Usually the change doesn't last very long.

Lasting change is made because people want to do something in a different way, and it usually comes from the inside. When we decide to think about changing our lives, it makes sense to take a good look at ourselves so that we can cope with our problems better than we have been doing instead of trying to get others to do all the work. When we work on ourselves and how we react to the situations around us, we take charge of our lives. Amazingly enough, if we make the changes within ourselves that we need to make, many times the people around us decide they will follow our example and change, too.

Problem-Solving for Young Adults

Problem-solving skills are not difficult to learn. They involve goal-setting, deciding on priorities, and brainstorming ideas about how to fix what is bothering us in our lives. In order to try out solutions, most of the time we need to learn to communicate effectively what we need and want from the people around us. These skills are useful to all young adults, not just those whose parents are divorcing. Although the following exercises focus on some of the problems faced by teenagers from homes where parents have divorced, the techniques work just as well with difficulties encountered in all types of families and in other situations, like school relationships with friends.

People who don't take the time to set goals tend to wander aimlessly. Before we can begin to think about how to get somewhere, we need to figure out just where it is we want to go. Otherwise, we'll get lost. Find some quiet time without distractions to imagine how you would like your family life to be. After you've thought about it for a while, write a brief description of what you came up with. If you feel more comfortable writing a list, that is fine, too.

Next write a short description or make a list of the way your family life is today. When you finish, read the two over and pick out the major differences between them. The discrepancies between how things are in our lives and the way we wish they could be aren't necessarily insurmountable problems. They could be opportunities that push us to be creative and force us to grow.

Some circumstances in our lives are givens. We can't change them, no matter how much we want to. Wishing we were taller or shorter, or that we had a different set of relatives, won't make those things happen. No matter how hard we try to change them, they stay the same. We can wear shoes with higher heels to look taller, or slump over to try to appear shorter, but we still are the same height we were before we did those things, and probably we didn't fool anybody for all our efforts. We can disown a pesky brother or sister, but in reality that person is still related to us.

Just as we can't change our height or our relatives, or even the fact that our parents may have chosen to divorce, we can't change anything that has happened to us before this very moment. Sometimes people spend too much time worrying about something they did weeks or months ago, or about something that others did that affected them— things that they can't undo unless they have a magic wand. Instead of working to change themselves in the here and now so they won't repeat their mistakes in the future, or so that the circumstances of their lives will be better, they play the "if-only" game. "If only I had studied for that math test, I wouldn't have flunked it," a person playing the if-only game might say, but he or she is too busy looking back to start studying for the next test.

When people who want to change the past aren't beating themselves up over what they've done, they're usually spending time blaming others and getting mad about what has been done to them. "If only my older sister hadn't gotten into a car wreck, then my parents would let me drive now," they might say, but they don't make the effort to be responsible. "If only my dad hadn't lost his job, then I would have enough money to buy the warm-up jacket I want," is an example of something you might hear people trapped in if-only thinking say, as they let themselves off the hook from figuring out ways they could earn money to start saving for the jacket they want.

Many times Selena thought, "If only my parents hadn't divorced, then everything would be going smoothly in my life and I would be happy." Maybe this was true, but probably not completely. Even if her parents had stayed together and their marriage was a good one, she would still have faced some disappointments in life not related to her family. Not everything would have turned out exactly the way she wanted it to, just as not every problem in her life now was caused by her parents' divorce. Some of the differences in the way your life is today, and how you want it to be, probably have little or nothing to do with your parents' divorce. Having to cope with challenges isn't something that is reserved only for teenagers whose parents have divorced.

Pull out your descriptions or lists again and look over those differences you noticed. See if you have included any items that, no matter how hard you work at it, you can't change because they are givens, or they are something that happened in the past. Cross those things off. Since you can't change them, you might as well stop worrying about them. Congratulations! Chances are you've made your first change—a change in attitude.

Now make yet another list—this time of the things in your life that you believe you can change. You may have many items on your list or you may have only a few. Pick one or two of them to begin working on. You might choose something that is bothering you most, or if that seems too overwhelming to tackle, then choose something that will be easier—a smaller-sized challenge that you can practice on.

Jeremy's list of what he wanted to work on looked like this:

How Things Are Now	How I Wish They Were
My parents try to get me involved in their arguments.	Let me stay out of it.
I don't have enough free time to do what I want to do.	I could stop doing chores.
Dad is late meeting us for visits.	That he got there on time.

Jeremy couldn't make his parents stop arguing or force them to stop trying to get him to take sides, so he didn't have a clue about how to solve that problem. Neither could he get by with doing nothing around the house—his mother wouldn't stand for that. There was no way he could make sure his dad got to the coffee shop on time, but he could change the way he reacted when he was in those situations. He decided to tackle the last problem on his list first.

First he sat down and talked with his father to let him know how important it was to him that he show up at the coffee shop when he promised he would. In order to increase the probability that his dad would listen to him, he picked a quiet and calm time and place where he could have his dad's complete attention.

Even though he was irritated at his father's habitual tardiness, Jeremy tried to keep anger out of what he said. Instead of accusing his father of always being late, or blaming him for making his children feel like he didn't care about the visits—both of which practically guaranteed he would have a fight on his hands—Jeremy said: "Dad, when you're late to pick us up, I start getting scared that you forgot about us." Even though he was tempted to blame his concern on his mother's temper, he knew that if his family situation was going to change, he had to start owning, and taking responsibility for, his own feelings.

His father didn't respond the way he wanted him to. In fact, he seemed to completely ignore what his son had said and asked him a question about the football game they were going to watch on T.V. Jeremy tried what counselors call the broken record technique. Slightly rephrasing what he'd just said, he repeated it, still careful not to blame his dad. "I really get nervous that you aren't going to pick us up, when you're late on Saturday mornings," he said. "Besides, I don't like having to get up early, when we have to wait for you for an hour." After a couple more tries, his father listened.

He said he hadn't known that his son felt anxious, but, since he worked hard all week, he was tired and sometimes when the alarm ran on Saturday morning, he slept right through it. He promised to try moving it across the room so that he would have to at least wake up enough to shut it off, and asked Jeremy to give him a wake-up phone call an hour before the time he was supposed to meet his children.

Jeremy was optimistic that the plan would work, but he knew there were no guarantees. Still he felt better because he'd made a major change just by talking with his dad, and not keeping his feelings to himself until they turned into resentments. Besides, he had another plan up his sleeve—if his father still was late, maybe he could try to get the times changed for the visits so that he wouldn't have to be disappointed or endure his mother's sputtering and his dad could still catch up on his rest. That way he could spend the hour he usually felt he wasted by waiting, either sleeping or doing something he wanted to do.

If his dad picked them up at noon on Saturday instead of eight in the morning, and dropped them off later on Sunday, maybe that would work. The only catch to that was that Jeremy's mother insisted that he and his sister come back to her house by dinnertime on Sundays to make sure they finished up their homework and got ready for school the next day. Maybe if he started taking his homework to his dad's house instead of waiting until the last minute to start it, she would agree to the time change. If not, he supposed he would have to learn to accept shorter visits with his father.

Next Jeremy decided to work on the housework problem. He knew his mom relied on him to help her out, but between her expectations, and time spent with his dad, he had little time left to sit and watch his favorite TV shows or just hang out with his friends. There was too much to do and too little time to do it in.

Before you read further think about what you would do to solve Jeremy's time problem. See if you can think of two or three different ideas he might try in order to get the time he needs to do the things he wants.

Some of the ideas Jeremy came up with were to

- try getting his homework done during study halls at school instead of wasting that time,
- get more organized about doing some of his chores,
- start urging his younger sister to do things like sort her own laundry and pick up after herself, and
- ask his mom if it would be okay to have a friend over after school so they could study together.

Once Jeremy had some ideas about how to change the way his life was going, he felt better. Even though he knew not every single one of them might work, at least he was doing something positive for himself instead of feeling sorry for himself as he'd tended to do in the past.

Now that you've looked at Jeremy's problem-solving strategies, try brainstorming some ways you might be able to improve some of the difficult situations in your life.

5

Coping with Special Problems

Some special situations faced by young adults whose parents divorce can cause them to feel as though their lives are turned inside out. Perhaps like Jeremy's mom and dad, their parents pull them into the middle of arguments, or expect them to take sides in a custody battle. Some parents move to another town or state, and a few cut off contact with their children altogether. Because of the stress divorce places on adults in the family, formerly mild-mannered parents may become so angry that they become verbally or even physically abusive. Others may react to stress by drinking too much or using drugs. Occasionally parents threaten to kidnap their own children from the custodial parent and, more often, mothers and fathers don't provide their children with financial support.

Even though these difficulties are more complicated than those caused by a parent who arrives late for visitation, or one who expects a child to take on too much responsibility,

all of the problems that teenagers with divorced parents
may face do have solutions. Some of the solutions are
more obvious than others, and some of them involve getting outside help. Even though teenagers can't control
what the adults in their lives are doing, they can learn to
recognize the unhealthy behaviors of others and take
steps to protect themselves from being harmed by them.

When Parents Want
Young People to Take Sides

Jeremy hated the fact that his mom and dad put him in the
middle when they argued, but they'd been doing it ever
since he could remember, and, realistically, he didn't think
they were about to change. He also suspected that they
needed help from a counselor in order to start communicating with each other better and leaving him and his sister out of their conflicts, but he knew they weren't ready
to hear that. If he brought the suggestion up, they would
hit the roof. Even though young people in Jeremy's situation can't stop the way their parents choose to handle their
disagreements with each other, they can protect themselves from the consequences of their parents' arguing.

First, young adults need to know that being asked to
take sides by warring parents is not good for their emotional well-being, and that taking sides certainly isn't a necessary part of being a loving child. Parents who force the
issue make their children suffer unnecessary loyalty conflicts. Even though a child loves both parents, he or she
may feel pressured to turn against one of them.

When parents such as Jeremy's expect their children to
side with them against the other parent, they also put their
children in what is called a no-win situation. No matter
what a teenager says or does, he or she is bound to make
at least one parent angry. Once their child has become a
major player in the conflict and learns to play parents

against each other in order to get what he or she wants, both parents become upset and quite frequently turn their anger on the young adult who already may feel like he or she is being torn in half.

Teenagers can survive parents' battles by realizing that no matter how hard their parents try to push or pull them into taking one side or another, and no matter how guilty they try to cause them to feel when they don't choose, young people don't have to take sides. The first thing a teenager can do is to stop responding when he or she is asked to take the side of one parent against the other, even if it means walking out of the room to avoid being part of the conversation.

A young person could let parents know how he or she feels by saying something like: "I care about both of you, and I don't want to take sides." Young adults can also let their parents know how being put in the position of having to choose one parent over another makes them feel by telling a parent: "I know you're angry at Dad (or Mom), but when you ask me to take sides, I feel confused/hurt/angry/worried."

The same holds especially in situations where parents draw their children into their legal battles as they vie for custody either in mediation or in the courts. Even though it is not fair to the other parent and certainly not to their children, some parents try to convince their offspring to play an active role in a legal custody battle. Because older children have more say in the court system about where they want to live, sometimes they face direct pressure from a parent to make a decision to live with him or her, or to give testimony that will lower the other parent's chances of obtaining court-appointed custody.

The best thing young people can do if they are feeling such pressure, is to be honest about their feelings and not hide them to please one of their parents or to keep Mom or Dad from getting angry or feeling hurt. If parents are fighting for custody and a young person does not have a preference about which parent he or she wants to live with, it is important to be clear about that, as well. In most custody disputes, unless the evidence is clearly weighted in favor of one parent, a court-appointed custody evaluation team consisting of a psychologist, a psychiatrist, and a social worker evaluates both parents and the children in order to make a recommendation.

Whether a family is evaluated by such a team, or a young person gets a chance to talk to the judge, or both, in most instances children are asked to state their preference in a private conversation without either parent present in order to make sure that they are being honest about what they want, not just trying to make their parents happy.

Some children and young adults are afraid that if they tell their true feelings, the parent they choose not to live with will retaliate by never wanting to see them again. Although sometimes this happens, it is rare for a parent to fight for custody and then abandon children if he or she loses, just as it is extremely rare for a judge to stop the non-custodial parent from having visitation rights. Usually, after the courts determine custody, visitations and relationships settle into a familiar pattern.

If parents continue to insist that their children take sides, and a teenager is having trouble sticking up for him- or herself, the young person can consider obtaining a lawyer to take care of his or her best interests. In many states, courts will appoint a lawyer for children involved in custody disputes if one is requested. This legal representative is called a *guardian ad litem*. Young people can find out whether their state has such a program by calling the court where the custody case will be heard.

When a Parent Moves Away

After two years of sharing custody with Bobbi's mother, her father's employer transferred him to another state halfway across the country. He didn't want to move, but it was necessary in order to keep his job. Because he was in a specialized field, he couldn't easily find another job that paid nearly as well. If he lost his job, his children would suffer financial hardship.

The day the movers came to pack up his belongings was sad for him, and for Bobbi and her brothers. Even though he reassured them that he would call often and that he would write, even though he promised them they would be spending Christmas vacation and most of summer vacation with him, she was upset by the change. She knew he was still her father and that they would continue have a relationship, but she didn't know what kind of a relationship it would be. She felt abandoned by him even though she knew he loved her and that he always would.

A young adult with a parent who moves far enough away so that visitation patterns change sometimes has a difficult time adapting to the new pattern. Just when he or she was getting used to life after the divorce, a whole new set of challenges come into play. More often than not, when a parent moves, a teenager will once again go through the grieving process, feeling shock, anger, denial, and sadness before he or she accepts the situation and learns to cope with it. The degree to which those feelings are experienced usually depends on how well the young person dealt with the challenging emotional issues during and soon after the divorce.

Even though maintaining a long-distance relationship with a parent without becoming emotionally distant isn't an easy task, it is possible. In most cases, when a parent moves, visits change. Instead of consistently seeing a parent frequently for relatively short periods of time, as Bobbi had been doing, children of divorce will spend longer periods of time with the parent who no longer lives close to them, and they will experience periods of separation, too. Not only do they need to come to terms with being away from the parent they no longer live with, they must learn to leave the comfort and security of their home for the longer visits.

Throughout the school year after her father moved, Bobbi missed him a great deal, but she did the best she could to keep him included in her life, so that he wouldn't forget her or wouldn't think she'd forgotten him. She sent him copies of her report card and pictures of her and her friends. When he was settled in his new job and had a computer at work, she E-mailed him from her school. That was more fun than writing letters, and it gave them a way to keep in closer contact. He called her every weekend. She felt bad when he called and she wasn't home, but she survived by looking forward to the day that school would end and she would fly to where he now lived to spend the summer with him.

As that time drew closer, something happened she hadn't counted on. Even though she couldn't wait to see her dad, she felt sad about leaving her mom for so long, longer than she'd ever done in her life. She worried about how her mother would cope without her and she wondered, sometimes, if her friends would forget her during the months she was away. It seemed as though she would have another set of long-distance relationships to maintain.

Even before she left for the airport, she felt homesick. Instead of crying, she avoided the whole issue of having to tell her mother good-bye by starting a fight over not doing the dishes when it was her turn. It was easier to turn her back on her mother and her home if she felt mad, than if she felt sad and scared. But as soon as she left to see her father, she felt bad about arguing with her mom. Once she'd arrived at her father's house, she was lonely again, and bored, because he couldn't spend all of his time with her—he had to work—and she hadn't made any friends there yet.

Eventually Bobbi learned to get used to longer visits and long-distance relationships, as most young adults do. Teenagers who find themselves trying to maintain a long-distance relationship with a parent can cope more easily if they

- do what they can to keep in contact with the parent who no longer lives nearby through phone calls and letters,
- keep in touch with the other parent and their own friends during longer visits,
- ask the parent they are visiting to help them get involved in organized activities, like sports groups, summer art classes, or clubs, so that they can more easily make friends,
- carry a "survival kit" that contains some good books or a hobby they can do if they get bored during visitations, as well as some small items that remind them of home,
- openly express their concerns to their parents, rather than acting them out, and
- ask for reassurances when they need them.

The Case of the Vanishing Parent

Even though it doesn't happen often, sometimes a non-custodial parent chooses to stop seeing his or her children after a divorce. There are several reasons why parents no longer want contact with their children. Children, except for the very youngest ones, have a difficult time accepting abandonment, and understanding that it is not their fault that their parent no longer wants to be around them. Instead, the decision to walk away without a backward glance comes from deep inside the parent. Teenagers need to be careful not to blame themselves for the abandonment. Self-blame leads to feelings of shame or being unworthy of love. In cases of abandonment, the shame rests with the parent, not the child who is left behind.

Some mothers and fathers never really bonded with their children in the first place. Perhaps their own parents did not have good parenting skills and were unable to raise them in a way that would enable them to be nurturing, caring parents as adults. Because they didn't have good role models as children, especially if a parent abandoned them, they never learned how to be emotionally or physically present for their children. Removing themselves from their children's lives after their marriage dissolved may seem normal to them, because that is what they experienced during their own growing-up years.

Alcohol and drug use can also cause parents to turn their backs on children. As we'll discuss later in this chapter, people who are dependent on alcohol or drugs give those substances top priority in their lives, placing them above relationships with people, even their own children. Although their intentions may be good, the urge to get high gets in the way of everything else. A parent who is chemically dependent may want to be around his or her children, but the job of being a parent somehow doesn't fit into a lifestyle that centers around nearly constant partying. Because alcohol and drugs lower people's inhibitions, a parent who is addicted to either of these substances may suddenly decide to move halfway across the country and forget to visit his or her children, or even call or write to them. Sometimes, parents who are addicted are so ashamed of themselves that they do not want their children to see them, so they remove themselves from their lives.

Occasionally a parent mistakenly believes that traveling back and forth between two households, and the loyalty conflicts that sometimes come from being in a bi-nuclear family, are just too painful to put his or her children through. The parent assumes that when two people break off their relationship as a married couple, their children must choose one parent over the other, and they tell themselves they will stop seeing their children in order not to put them through the emotional pain of having to make such a choice.

In truth, children experience more pain when they feel that a parent is rejecting them. Most parents who have nothing more to do with their children, and say they are doing it for the good of their children, are making an excuse to cover up the real reason that they no longer want to have contact with them. Often they are the ones who experience pain and feelings of abandonment when their children leave after a visit, and for one reason or another they have a difficult time dealing with their own sadness and sense of loss.

A few parents stop seeing their children out of anger at losing a custody battle. They are all-or-nothing thinkers who do not believe in compromise. Either they will have full custody of their children, or they want nothing to do with them. Their children, simply because they won't take the angry parent's side, become a focus for rage at the ex-spouse who divorced them. These parents tell themselves that their children are just like the other parent, or that parent has poisoned the children's minds against them and use that as an excuse to stop visitations. They are angry and hurt and want to make someone else hurt just as much. It is unfortunate that they pick on their children as targets.

Some parents, like Selena's father, may stop seeing their children when they become involved in another romantic relationship. Some parents do get so swept up in a new relationship that they focus entirely on that to the exclusion of their children. Believing that they can have a completely new life and a fresh start, they don't want their children around, because they serve as uncomfortable reminders of the past relationship. Even though non-custodial parents may use the excuse that the man or woman they are involved with doesn't like children, or doesn't like *their* children, the decision to stop seeing their children is one that they alone have made; a romantic partner can't force them into it. Fortunately for Selena, her father changed his mind and started spending time with her again.

As we discussed in Chapter Two, young adults whose parents remove themselves from their lives have a more difficult time adjusting to divorce than do other teenagers who have both parents choosing to remain central in their lives. Being abandoned by a parent is a major loss. The grieving process that must be gone through in order to heal from that loss is more intense and often lasts quite a bit longer than does the grief of teenagers with a parent who moved across town or down the street.

Life is not always fair. Even though it isn't easy to adjust to being abandoned by a parent, one way of looking at the situation is to know that if all a parent can give a child is to help begin his or her life, that, in itself, is still a big gift. The child must be meant to be living on this earth because, if they weren't, they wouldn't be here. There are always other caring adults who are able to give a young person the guidance and nurturing a parent can't or won't.

Verbal and Physical Abuse

Adults who are stressed out by the breakup of their relationship and the divorce process may grow short-tempered. Their children, who are under stress as well, can become quick-tempered too. Parents who are having trouble dealing with their emotional issues, and having a difficult time controlling their anger, sometimes say mean things to their children. Everyone occasionally says sharp words to others they wish they hadn't spoken when they were angry. The angry words may take the shape of a threat or a put-down. While occasional angry words aren't a good thing, they are normal. When threats and put-downs become a pattern, they turn into verbal or emotional abuse.

Because it doesn't leave physical scars, verbal abuse can be a difficult thing to recognize and resolve. When Jeremy's mother kept telling him that he was a no-good bum just like his father whenever he disagreed with her, or dragged his feet when it came to doing chores, he began to wonder if he really was no-good. Teenagers who are called stupid, lazy, ugly, or bad just because they happen to be in the wrong place at the wrong time, and become the target of a parent's anger, often blame themselves instead of placing responsibility for the outburst on the verbal abuser. They internalize the bad things that are said about them, believing that they really are stupid, lazy, ugly, or bad.

Emotional and verbal abuse includes

- threats of violence, such as: "If you don't turn that music down, I'm going to come in there and slap you."
- implied threats of violence like balled up fists, pacing back and forth, or other signs that indicate a person's temper is not under control,
- violence against property, such as smashing a stereo or cutting up clothing,
- mental cruelty in the form of insults and put-downs often said in front of others.

"You made me so mad, I couldn't help myself," Jeremy's mother told him after she had threatened to kick him out of the house for folding the towels wrong the day after she'd been arguing all week with her ex-husband over money. Like Jeremy's mom, verbal abusers don't take responsibility for their actions, just as they don't take responsibility for their feelings. Rather than admitting that they made a mistake when they insulted someone or threatened them, they tend to either blame the person they lashed out at, or find another reason to excuse their behavior, such as having a bad day.

Even though it doesn't leave physical scars, verbal abuse leaves emotional ones that can hurt victims just as much as hitting and slapping do. Although federal child abuse laws do cover severe emotional abuse, because verbal abuse is often hidden and hard to prove, and because victims tend to blame themselves, many young adults suffer it in silence.

If a young person believes that he or she is being verbally abused by a parent, the best thing to do is to see a counselor, either at school or through a mental health service. Together, the young person and the counselor can work out strategies to help make the situation better at home by stopping the abuse, or finding a way to leave the abusive situation, and work to strengthen the teenager's self-esteem.

Some parents do more than threaten—they lash out with physical violence. According to 1996 statistics collected from child protection agencies by the U.S. Department of Health and Human Services, almost 1 million children under 18 were victims of child abuse and neglect that year. They were abandoned or punched, beaten, kicked, bitten, burned, or shaken. Researchers believe that child abuse happens much more often than the statistics indicate because many cases are not reported to agencies.

When most people think of child abuse, they picture young children who are beaten, and they assume that it doesn't happen to teenagers because they can take care of themselves. That is far from the truth. Although the majority of physically abused children are younger, teenagers can and do become victims of violence. Twenty-one percent of reported child abuse cases in 1995 were young people between the ages of 13 and 18.

Physical violence is something no child should have to endure, even though a parent may excuse his or her hurtful actions by claiming they are going through a rough time because of the divorce. If a parent becomes physically violent to a young adult or to a brother or sister, it is important to get help immediately, because physical abuse can be a matter of life and death. In 1995, nearly a thousand children died as the result of child abuse.

Young people who feel frightened about calling a child protection agency, or the local police or sheriff's department (all of which are listed in the telephone book), should tell a teacher or a school counselor so that they can report what is happening to the proper authorities, who can stop the abuse before it is too late.

If Mom or Dad Drinks or Uses Drugs

Many adults who are working their way through a divorce go through what people jokingly call the divorce crazies. They may start wearing a different style of clothing, change their hair style, and get a different group of friends. Stay-at-home parents might start going out. Like teenagers, they are trying on a new identity. In their attempt to figure out who they are as individuals rather than as part of a couple, they may go through a period of partying.

For some parents, that means drinking or drug use. An adult might take a few drinks before going out, or light up a joint, because they've forgotten how it was to find someone to date or how to be sociable, and they believe that alcohol relaxes them and helps them to relate to others. Because alcohol lowers their inhibitions, they think it gives them courage, and they use it like a crutch. Sometimes single parents begin drinking more, or using drugs, because they want to temporarily escape their emotional pain and feelings of rejection.

Many adults who are putting their lives back together after a divorce find a happy medium after a brief time of experimenting, but some parents really do seem to go off the deep end when it comes to alcohol or drugs. They drift into a lifestyle that includes abuse of chemical substances, and in time become emotionally and sometimes physically dependent on alcohol or drugs.

Instead of drinking alcohol or smoking marijuana to have a good time and temporarily forget their problems, they drink or take drugs just to feel normal and get through the day. In the meantime, their children's lives seem anything but normal.

Selena's mom didn't really think about what she was doing; she didn't pay attention to the fact that she needed to drink more and more in order to get through the evening so she could get to sleep, and to sleep through the night. At first Selena didn't notice the increase in her mother's drinking either, but soon it became clear that something was radically wrong. Her mom would promise to do things like sign permission slips for field trips and then forget them, she was difficult to talk with, and often she was grouchy. Eventually Selena grew embarrassed at the thought of bringing her friends home because she never knew how her mother would be on the weekends or at night.

Alcohol and drug dependency affect not only the person who is addicted, but their children as well. The more dependent a person becomes on a substance, the less time and energy they have to devote to being a parent. Alcohol and drug addiction make it impossible to be a good parent, because people who depend on these substances focus all their attention on where the next drink or pill is coming from.

Home life for young people who are children of alcoholic- or drug-dependent parents is unpredictable, even more unpredictable than the changes families experience right after a divorce. Children raised in single-parent families are sometimes asked to take on many more responsibilities than they are used to. The pressure to act like an adult is increased in homes where alcohol or drug dependency is present. Young adults often need to fill adult roles in order to keep the home and family functioning. Because they negatively affect a person's self-control, alcohol and drugs play a role in child abuse and neglect, and in incest as well.

Young adults whose parents abuse alcohol or drugs often try to get them to stop using by hiding their chemical of choice, arguing with their parent, or trying to make Mom or Dad feel guilty. None of these tactics work. If a parent has an alcohol or drug problem, it is important to get professional help. No one can make another person stop drinking or using drugs until the person is willing to quit, but young adults can make their own lives better, and they can learn ways to stop making it easy for a parent to continue the drinking and drugging. Nearly every community has Alanon and Alateen groups that help people who love alcoholics master these skills. These organizations are listed in the telephone book.

Child-Snatching

Very few parents become so enraged by a divorce or so lonely for full-time contact with their children that they kidnap or abduct them, but a few do. According to statistics provided by the U.S. Department of Justice, as many as 350,000 children were abducted by parents in 1988. As a result of increasing awareness and stronger law enforcement, that figure has more than likely dropped during the last decade. Canadian figures from the Royal Canadian Mounted Police show that 2 percent of the children who are listed as missing in that country are victims of child-snatching, also called parental kidnapping.

Information gathered by the Royal Canadian Mounted Police from kidnappings in Canada and the United States indicates that both mothers and fathers abduct children. The agency collected information in both countries to help prevent child-snatching. While mothers tend to take children after the court awards custody to the father, fathers who kidnap their children most often do so before court decisions are made—perhaps fearing that they will lose the custody fight.

Children who are taken by their parents are usually abducted from their homes rather than from places like schools or day care centers. In most cases, parents do not use physical force; their children willingly accompany them, and probably are unaware that they are being kidnapped. Most children who are child-snatching victims are between three and seven years of age, and most cases of child-snatching are resolved within a week, because frequently the parent who has the children communicates with the other parent, and uses the children as hostages to win an argument or force a reconciliation.

The reasons that a parent may kidnap children are many. According to one study, the most common is to get revenge on the other parent. Some parents take children to get the other partner to chase them. Both of these reasons have more to do with the relationship between the two adults than with parents' love for their children. Some parents who take their children are emotionally troubled. Others believe the judge made a mistake by granting custody to the other parent. The final reason parents kidnap their own children is that they are concerned for their safety. They have reason to believe the other parent has physically or sexually abused their children, or has threatened it, and the courts did nothing to protect the children.

In the United States, the Uniform Child Custody Jurisdiction Act, which has been adopted by every state, makes custodial kidnapping illegal. This law says that if a parent keeps a child contrary to a court order, or takes a child from the custodial parent, he or she will face criminal charges. It was passed to discourage parents from abducting their children and taking them across state lines to avoid being caught.

In addition, a 1980 U.S. law, the Parental Kidnapping Prevention Act, requires each state to honor the custody orders that are issued by other states. Once the decision has been made, a parent can't take the child to another state and try to get the first judge's decision reversed. These two laws apply both to temporary and to permanent custody orders. In Canada, Sections 282 and 283 of the Criminal Code serve the same function. Divorce Act child custody orders are valid and can be enforced throughout the country.

Children whose non-custodial parent takes them from the custodial parent and hides them, or refuses to let the other parent have contact with them, are placed in a very difficult situation.

Although he never carried through with his threat, soon after the divorce Jeremy's father said that he had half a mind to take Jeremy and his sister to another state without telling their mother where they had gone. Usually he talked this way right after Jeremy's mom had threatened to cut off his visitation rights, and once the visits resumed, he wouldn't mention his plan—until the next time she withheld contact with his children from him.

Even though he knew his dad was probably making idle threats, they made Jeremy worry. If his father made good on his threat, what would he do? Sometimes he stayed awake nights thinking about it. If his dad started packing, he could call his mother, but then she would call the police and his dad would be thrown in jail. If he kept quiet, maybe he would never see his mom again. Jeremy was lucky because his father didn't carry through with his plans.

Other young adults aren't so fortunate. If a parent tries to convince a young adult to disappear and to help take younger children in the family in order to get revenge, or to try to get back together with the other parent, going along with it is a very bad idea, no matter how convincing the parent doing the kidnapping may be. It is a plan that will hurt both parents. Chances are, the parent who doesn't know where the children are will be frantic with worry. The parent who takes the children risks fines and jail time as well as the possibility of seeing children only during supervised visits.

Child-snatching hurts the children too. Even though being on the run may seem exciting at first, especially for teenagers who are angry at the parent they are running from, the reality of life on the run is usually far different later on. Parents who have taken their children often can't work because they will be asked for Social Security numbers, and often must move frequently in order to avoid detection. Children have to assume different names and may be unable to attend school or even to have friends. Living that way is a high price to pay for teaching a parent a lesson.

In instances in which the court really has made a mistake in granting custody, or where sexual or physical abuse, or drugging or drinking are involved, unless the danger from contact with a parent is life-threatening, there are better ways to resolve the problem than running away. These include contacting social service agencies and police, or obtaining professional advice from a lawyer.

If a parent threatens or begins making plans to illegally take a young adult or younger brothers and sisters from the custodial parent, it is important that the teenager talk about what is going on with a trusted adult. If a parent asks a teenager to go along, the young person can try to talk him/her out of it by helping him/her understand the consequences of child-snatching. Young people have a right to refuse to go, even if it means disobeying a parent. They also have a right to contact law enforcement authorities if their parent kidnaps them or their siblings.

No Child Support

According to the United States Census Bureau about half of the custodial parents, 6.2 million of them, in the United States receive child support. Fifty-six percent of them were mothers as of 1992, according to the most recent figures. About three quarters of the divorced women received at least some money, but only 63 percent of the women who were supposed to make payments to fathers, made them. In 1991 fathers who did not receive child support payments had average incomes of $18,144. Mothers who didn't receive the payments averaged $14,602 in income. Most child support that was awarded did not require the non-custodial parent to provide health insurance.

When a parent refuses to pay court-ordered child support, his or her decision makes life hard for the children, who often must do without many of the basic necessities of life. This is especially difficult to tolerate if the parent who won't pay has a steady job, and a standard of living that is much more comfortable than that of his or her children. Even when a parent has a good reason not to pay— like losing a job—non-payment causes difficulties for children.

Soon after he was transferred, Bobbi's father's new company downsized, cutting back on employees. Those who had been hired last were the first to be laid off—including Bobbi's father. Although he was eligible for unemployment, it took time to process his paperwork, and even when the checks started coming, there was barely enough to pay his own living expenses. He sent Bobbi's mother what he could, and said that he felt bad about not being able to send more. Bobbi understood that her father was looking for a job and that by no means was he a deadbeat dad, but she felt angry when she couldn't afford the school shoes she wanted after her old ones wore out. She felt angry at herself for feeling upset, as well, because she knew her having to do without wasn't his fault. She couldn't help but think, though, that if her parents hadn't gotten divorced, her life would be easier.

Sometimes, parents who have been ordered to pay child support express their anger at the custodial parent by refusing to pay anything toward helping to pay their children's expenses. This causes not only financial problems, but emotional hardships for children and young adults, who feel doubly abandoned. It may seem to them that their well-being isn't important to their parent at all. When a parent takes such extreme measures to teach another parent a lesson, it is the children who suffer.

When children's expenses or a parent's income changes, either the parent with custody or the parent making the payments can bring the child support order before a judge and have it modified or changed to reflect the changing circumstances of the family members.

In the United States, under the Uniform Child Support Act, all children have a right to financial help from both parents. In Canada, the Divorce Act guarantees children the same right. If a parent refuses to pay, the other parent can obtain help in getting the order enforced through government social service agencies, legal aid offices, or private attorneys.

6

Living Happily
Ever After

Even though at the beginning many teenagers feel that nothing positive can come from their parents' divorce, the shake-up that has occurred gives both parents and their older children an opportunity to look at the way they want to live, and to make good choices about how to continue on with their lives. Although life in a single-parent home is usually very different than when two parents are present, eventually young people who have been affected by a divorce find their lives calm down as new patterns emerge both within themselves, and in their daily lives. One of these new patterns is a more independent way of living.

When Bobbi's father moved away and then lost his job, there wasn't enough money for her needs. When her class took a field trip to a movie, she had a difficult time coming up with the money for a ticket. Her tennis racquet broke, and she couldn't afford to get it restrung. If her friends went to the mall, she stayed home because she didn't even have money to buy a soda.

At first she sat around feeling sorry for herself, but when a friend suggested she check at the school guidance office to see if a counselor could get her a part-time job, Bobbi jumped at the chance. Her mom said it was fine as long as she worked to bring up her grades and didn't put off doing her homework. Soon she was working three hours a day after school at a day care center, helping with children and preparing snacks. Even though the check she brought home wasn't a big one, it was enough for her to buy what she needed, and she could afford other things she wanted, like some new clothes, as well.

The best thing about her job was that working at the day care center didn't seem like a job to her at all, she enjoyed it so much. Mrs. Carver, the woman who ran the center, was interesting to talk with and Bobbi was surprised at how much fun the job was. She began thinking about taking early childhood development classes when she finished high school and that maybe she would run a day care center of her own someday.

Different Households, Different Rules

Often when two parents live together in one home, their ideas about how their children ought to be raised are not alike. Because they are married and working together as a team, most parents try to compromise over issues such as what the children should be allowed to eat, how late they can stay up at night, and what happens to a child who is disobedient. When parents are no longer married, they still have to compromise over some things, but how their children are expected to conduct themselves in their home is up to each individual parent. With two households, usually there are two sets of rules. Since young adults are part of both households, and must travel back and forth between them, two sets of rules can be confusing to them.

When Selena stayed at her father's house on weekends, she didn't have to do any chores, because his girlfriend did them all. Selena didn't even have to clean her room, because she slept on the sofa in her dad's tiny apartment. Her mother didn't care about how much TV she watched and how long she talked on the phone, but her dad set limits.

For a while, it seemed as if she was always getting into trouble. She'd get used to sleeping late at her father's and not helping out, and then when she went back with her mom and did the same thing, her mother would hit the roof and call her lazy. She was only human. It wasn't fun to do chores. When she told her mom, "Well, my dad lets me sleep until noon and I don't have to do dishes there," her mom got even angrier. Much the same thing happened when she told her father that her mom let her watch as much TV as she wanted.

Selena was fortunate because the rules in her parents' homes were fairly straightforward. She didn't have to play guessing games about what her mother or her father expected. They were clear about what they wanted, and if she didn't meet their expectations about how she should be acting, they wasted no time in telling her about it.

Other young adults aren't so lucky. They find themselves in situations where a parent, especially one who isn't used to taking primary responsibility for raising children, is still learning how to be a parent. In other instances, a parent may be suddenly so overwhelmed by the emotional, practical, and financial demands of the divorce, that he or she doesn't have much time to focus on skills like discipline or offering guidance. These households may appear not to have any rules at all, but in truth, they do. The rules are there but they are unspoken. Usually when young people break the unspoken rules, their behavior is met with anger. To survive life in two households with separate sets of rules, young adults sometimes need to take the initiative and ask parents what they expect so their understanding of the rules will be clear.

Sometimes Bobbi felt like she was walking on eggshells when she was with her dad. He was a naturally quiet person and always seemed to get along with everybody. She could tell sometimes when she did or said certain things that she disappointed him, because then he got really quiet. The problem was that often she didn't have a clue about what she'd done that he considered wrong. Sometimes it made her nervous because he was her father and she wanted to please him. If she wasn't sure about how he wanted her to behave, how could she do that? After they had a talk, everything was fine.

Even when teenagers know how their parents want them to behave, they often test the rules just to see what they can get away with. When they misbehave, their parents set limits on their behavior. This is normal. Even though young people may rebel against the rules, having them is necessary because knowing that they are there offers children of all ages a sense of security. They know that their parents care enough about them to set expectations for them.

Sometimes when a non-custodial parent feels guilty about the divorce and his or her lack of constant contact with the children, that mother or father is reluctant to set any rules at all, and he or she may try to buy a young person's affections, falling into the trap of what some people call being a Disneyland Mom or Dad. Although having a parent spend money on you and never set limits on your behavior may seem like a dream come true at first, later on the reality may not be quite so wonderful.

Several months after he divorced her mother, Selena's father felt bad about neglecting his daughter right after the divorce took place. Even though he still refused to pay the court-ordered child support, he said that he wanted Selena to get over being angry at him, and tried to make it up to her for the times he didn't see her. At first it was fun, getting him to take her to the mall. He bought her expensive sweaters and, even though her mother didn't allow her to wear much make-up, her father would purchase anything she wanted at the cosmetic counter. When a new CD came out and she wanted it, she didn't have to think twice about who to ask. Her dad would pull out his checkbook next time she visited him.

In the beginning, having nearly anything her heart desired made her feel good, but after a while she wanted something more from her father than his presents. If only he would just sit down and talk with her about how her school was going and try to get to know her better, she thought. She'd gladly trade some of her clothes and CDs for that. Besides, it felt really strange to go back home to her mother's and have to worry about whether there would be food in the refrigerator. Lately, she'd become an expert at putting off collectors when they called about her mom's bills. The simple truth was they didn't have enough money to live on. Because he let her do nearly anything she wanted when she stayed at his house, Selena began to question how much her dad really cared about her.

Sure, she got mad at her mom when she wouldn't let her stay up all night watching videos, and told her not to eat junk food. It made her very angry when her mother got bossy and tried to choose her friends. Even so, she knew her mom was doing what she thought was best for her and that, even when she was meddlesome, she was interfering out of love. Sometimes, because he didn't seem to care what happened to her, just that she got her way, Selena questioned whether or not her father loved her. It seemed more important to him that she love him—no matter what the cost.

The best course of action when a parent tries to buy love, or won't ever say no out of fear of disappointing a son or daughter, is to try not to manipulate and take advantage of the situation because, no matter how tempting that may be, it only hurts the relationship in the long run.

Eventually Selena's dad felt resentful about her because wherever he saw her, she expected him to give her money, and her demands kept increasing. Selena was mad at her father because he was the one who had set up the situation in the first place. He was the one who had acted as though being a good father only meant buying things. If he didn't like the way things were going between them, he should just put his checkbook away, she thought, and not walk around grumbling all the time.

The resentments on both sides grew until Selena gathered enough courage to talk with him directly about her feelings. She told him how important he was to her and that, even though there were a lot of things she wanted, just spending time with him was enough. At first he acted shocked to hear such adult words come from his daughter, but he smiled and told her he hadn't known how she felt before. He'd been trying the best he could to make her happy.

When the boundless giving and the limitless living stop, there are bound to be rough spots to overcome as parents and teenagers find new ways of relating to each other. Some young adults have a difficult time giving up the idea that they can get a parent to give in to their demands by threatening to withhold love from them. Some adults find it very difficult to risk a child's temporary anger by saying no, or they may go overboard the other way for a time and be too strict, and even stingy.

Usually a parent who has tried to please his or her children by allowing them to do as they want, and buying them whatever they ask for, gets tired of living that way as time goes on. As children and their non-custodial parent spend more time together, the situation gradually changes. Parents realize that all homes need rules and all children need discipline. They start to understand, as well, that love between parents and children isn't based on how much a single parent can buy for his or her sons and daughters. Even though it feels good to give and receive presents, that is only a small part of the relationship, and doesn't take away the hurt feelings caused by divorce.

Becoming the "Man" or "Woman" of the House

Studies of young people whose parents divorce uniformly show that they tend to take on more responsibility for themselves and for their families. Young adults may assume a greater number of chores around the house, and might have to spend more time babysitting younger brothers and sisters than they ever did before. When money is short, older teenagers, like Bobbi, sometimes find themselves having to go to work at a part-time job in order to buy clothing or school supplies. They may even start helping out with expenses around the home.

Although taking on so many new responsibilities can cause resentment at the lack of free time, most teenagers want to be helpful, so they do the best they can. Some teenagers, however, are called upon to do too much. At a time in their lives when they need to start forging their identities as independent individuals, and are beginning to break away from the family, they get so caught up in meeting their parents' needs and those of their brothers and sisters that they don't have time for lives of their own.

When Jeremy's father moved out, his mother said that he was now the "man of the family." That made him feel uncomfortable because he knew there was no way he could do all of the things his father had done, especially making decisions that would affect the whole family. For a while, it seemed like his mom asked him for advice on everything from what to do about health insurance to whether to try to get a new car or fix the old one when the mechanic told her it needed a valve job.

Luckily for him, she noticed that such questions made him really nervous, and that the more responsibility she heaped on his shoulders, the more time he spent alone in his room with his headphones on trying to avoid it. When she asked him what was wrong, he told her that he just wasn't ready for what she expected of him. He wished he could make good decisions of the type she needed, but he didn't have the answers. He told her that maybe it would be better if she asked one of his uncles for advice. Even though they lived in different parts of the country, they could help her more over the telephone than Jeremy could in person because they knew more.

He was relieved when she agreed to his suggestion, and admitted that there were many things she would need to learn about that she'd always relied on his father for before. She apologized to her son for asking him to fill his father's shoes without really thinking of the consequences. She even decided to sign up for a non-credit car maintenance class through adult education at the local high school, just so she could learn some basics and be able to talk to mechanics on her own.

Even though taking on some new responsibilities is a necessary part of living in a single-parent home, big problems can arise when parents ask their young adults for help that is not emotionally healthy for them to provide. As Selena's mother started to do soon after her husband left, parents sometimes begin acting as if their children were adult friends instead of their children. Sometimes parents inappropriately share the most intimate details of their lives with their children—burdening them with things they would rather not know—because they don't have a counselor or a support network of adult friends to talk with. Young people placed in this position may be asked to help their parents make personal choices that young people should have no responsibility for at all.

Selena didn't want to hear her mother's complaints about her dad. Not only did listening when she talked that way spark loyalty conflicts, it made Selena feel responsible for finding solutions to the problems that were causing her mother's sadness and anger. When her mom would ask her a question like, "What do you think is so wrong with me that your father would need to go out and get another woman?" or "Do you think I should go out with his best friend and teach him a lesson?" she put her daughter in a very difficult position. Not only did Selena not know the answers to her mother's questions, under the pretense of asking for her advice, her mother was manipulating her to take sides against her father.

Being forced to act like an adult before becoming one causes a role reversal, parents acting like children and forcing children to act like parents. Role reversals turn families upside down. Often mothers and fathers aren't aware that the advice and emotional nurturing they may be expecting from their children is unreasonable and inappropriate, especially if they aren't taking care of their emotional needs, or don't have a good support network. Like Selena's mom, their judgment may be clouded by alcohol or drugs.

Although Jeremy's mother kept her demands on her son at a practical level, wanting him to make decisions about finances and the car, some parents expect a teenage son or daughter to fill the role of their ex-spouse in nearly every way except sexually. This kind of adult-to-adult emotional intimacy with a lonely parent is called emotional incest by mental health professionals. A young adult son or daughter who has been chosen to become an emotional substitute for a parent's adult partner may feel very special or helpful. Growing very close to a parent may also feel comforting coming at a time when a teenager has many unanswered questions about his or her family's future.

Relationships like these are not healthy for the parent or for his or her children, because they prevent teenagers from forming and maintaining healthy boundaries—the line where they leave off and the other person begins. Neither the parent nor the child has privacy. Healthy love between parents and children encourages young people to begin building an independent life of their own, which doesn't include having to build a parent's self-esteem or nurture them. Emotional incest encourages teenagers to become so tightly enmeshed with a parent that they miss out on growing up.

Sometimes talking with a parent helps, as does setting limits and sticking to them. In other instances, letting a parent know you are unwilling to give him or her emotional advice, or to give up your friendships in order to be emotionally available to him or her isn't enough. Some parents cannot see that the emotional relationship they demand of their children isn't healthy because of the way they grew up, or because of their need to depend on other people to help them feel good about themselves.

If a parent still clings to them too tightly, expecting young adults to act like parents in the relationship, or puts demands on them to be too emotionally intimate, there is little they can do on their own to change the situation. In that case, young people need to talk the problem over with a health professional such as a school counselor or social worker who may be able to set up family counseling sessions.

It doesn't happen all of the time, but neither is it unusual for emotional incest to develop sexual overtones. Sometimes the result is that a parent demands sexual closeness with a young adult. Although incest most often occurs between fathers and daughters, mothers have been known to force their sons to perform sexual acts as well. Parents who initiate sexual relationships with their children do them major emotional damage.

Incest is sexual abuse. Its effects can haunt children and young adults for a lifetime. If you feel a parent is acting seductively, pressuring, manipulating or trying to force you to share a sexual relationship, there is no need to suffer silently in an attempt to protect your parent. Seek outside help by talking with a teacher, a school counselor, or a social worker from your local social services department.

When Mom or Dad Dates

Most single parents eventually begin dating. Just because Mom or Dad starts having a social life doesn't mean wedding bells will ring in his or her future, but it might. Many divorced people do find another partner to love, and they remarry. In the United States at least one of the partners in 40 percent of all marriages has been married before, according to U.S. Census figures. Sixty-five percent of those marriages include children from a previous relationship.

Several months after the divorce was final, Jeremy's father joined a single-parent group that held picnics, skating trips, and other events for divorced or widowed parents and their children. He told his son that it was a good way for him and his sister to make new friends, and that he would enjoy meeting and talking with other single parents. The group would be like a support group for him. Jeremy didn't mind going to the meetings. In fact, he felt comforted about what had happened in his family by being around other kids going through the same adjustments he was. They seemed to be doing fine in their lives, and he sensed that as time went on he would be too.

When he saw his father striking up more and more conversations with a tall, red-haired woman with two young daughters, Jeremy didn't mind. His dad was an adult; he deserved a life. Besides, he kind of liked Clarissa—that was her name. She was good at pitching a soft ball and she brought some mean chili to the potlucks. Her jokes were funny, too. When his dad began inviting Clarissa and her daughters over to his house for pizza and to watch videos on the weekends Jeremy and his sister visited, he wasn't so sure he liked her anymore.

His emotions confused him, especially after a few weeks into his father's new relationship, when it became obvious that Clarissa and his dad were far more than just friends. Jeremy found himself feeling disloyal to his mom for liking Clarissa, and angry at his father because, even though he knew his dad was divorced and had every right to have a girlfriend, it still felt to him like his father was playing around behind his mother's back. He resented how, when all of them were together, this new woman took much of his father's attention, and how it took all the strength he had to hold himself back from blowing up when his dad seemed to pay more attention to Clarissa's girls than his own children. He suspected his father was doing that to impress his new girlfriend. Even though he knew it was wrong, he began cooking up schemes about how to drive her away so things would be the way they were before.

Learning to tolerate and get along with a parent's new romantic partner is a process that can take some interesting twists and turns. Because Selena's father had ignored visitations altogether right after he left her mother and was caught up in his new relationship, it took Selena a long time to have any friendly feelings toward the woman with whom he now shared his life. Besides, she didn't want to get too attached because she was afraid the two of them might break up and she'd have to go through another loss.

Younger teens sometimes get upset at a parent's dating because they see their mothers and fathers only as parents. That role doesn't include falling in love or possibly having sex. Because older teens are more independent and in the process of coming to terms with their own sexuality, they often react differently. The fact that a parent may be starting a new relationship may not be all that threatening to them. They have begun to think of their parents as individuals with lives beyond the role of parent. Since young adults are starting to be interested in romantic relationships themselves, the idea that a parent might want to be emotionally and physically intimate with another person doesn't come as a total shock.

Even so, young people of all ages can still feel jealous about another person taking a parent's time and attention. Selena didn't expect to be the center of her mother's universe, and she was glad that her mom had needs and interests that didn't include her. She was especially happy when her mother stopped drinking and began attending Alcoholics Anonymous meetings. When her mom began talking about a man she met at a sobriety dance, however, Selena felt like she was being abandoned. Between her mother's work and school and the new social life, the time they spent together seemed to shrink.

Often a parent's dating triggers loyalty conflicts along with other unresolved emotional issues surrounding the divorce. Unexpressed anger and sadness or worry may resurface once more and need to be dealt with. When a parent starts dating, young people must once and for all give up the notion that their mother and father will make up, get back together, and live happily ever after. This can come as a shock, especially if they never admitted to themselves that they fantasized that everything would go back the way it was before the divorce. Since they haven't worked their way through the grief process, they need to spend time doing that.

The way parents handle their dating relationships also affects how young people will adjust to this new circumstance. Just because a parent feels attracted to another person, doesn't guarantee that his or her children will feel the same way. Although some parents try to keep their dating life separate from their children, others don't. They include their sons and daughters in activities with the new partner, like Jeremy's father did. Some even ask the person they are dating to sleep over during times when their children are present in the home. It isn't unusual for teenagers and younger children to have difficulty accepting this arrangement.

Young people have an easier time if romantic partners are introduced gradually, and they aren't expected to relate to them as a step-parent or substitute parent. Life with a dating parent is easier, as well, when that parent makes sure that he or she maintains quality time alone with the children, rather than using the new love interest as a babysitter or insisting that everyone spend visitations together as "one big, happy family."

Parents have a right to form relationships with other adults and to expect that their friends, both romantic and otherwise, be treated with courtesy and respect. Teenagers have a right to hold their own opinions about a parent's friend and to decide for themselves the level of closeness they want with that person.

Hiding feelings doesn't work for very long because they are bound to come out somehow—usually in inappropriate ways. When young people feel discomfort at a parent's dating, they need to talk openly about their feelings in a private discussion with the parent. It is okay for young adults to ask questions and to let parents know what they need in order to feel better about what is happening.

When Jeremy and his father talked, he was relieved to learn that his dad wasn't planning a wedding. He agreed to be more polite to Clarissa and her daughters, but he told his father that he still needed time alone with him like they'd had before. Jeremy's dad agreed.

Finding Adult Role Models

Single parents often say that they are expected to be both mother and father to their children. Sometimes it may feel that way, but no matter how hard a single parent may try, he or she simply can't be both mother and father. Studies show that in order to grow up to be healthy adults children need both male and female role models.

Men provide certain things for children and women provide other things, because the experience of being a man and of being a woman are very different—even beneath sex-role stereotyping imposed by society. For instance, having a healthy relationship with a father increases a girl's sense of self-esteem and influences her to make positive choices in future relationships with men as she grows older. She learns how to have healthy relationships with men from her father. Boys learn how to relate to women from their mothers. Fathers serve as role models for boys. By watching their fathers and interacting with them, boys learn what it means to be men and to feel good about themselves, just as girls learn similar lessons by being around their mothers.

Single-parent families present a challenge, because even when custody is shared, the contact that a young person has with each parent is diminished. During the times a son or daughter is staying at Dad's house, Mom isn't around, and during the times he or she is staying at Mom's house, Dad usually isn't present. When one parent is awarded sole custody and the other parent visitation, children find the time they spend with the parent they do not live with greatly decreases. On the positive side, when young adults visit a parent as the result of divorce, the time they spend together will probably be filled with more quality time than would normally occur during the same time period in a two-parent home. Because their time together is limited, children of divorce and their parents usually plan activities together and spend more time talking with each other.

Even though divorce cuts back on the amount of time that children spend with one or both parents, it doesn't have to create an impossible situation or leave major gaps in their development. After all, in homes where both parents are present, they are rarely available for their children most of the time. School and work schedules cut into time, and even when everyone is home together they aren't always interacting. Mom may be making a shopping list or finishing up work she brought home from the office. Dad may be talking on the phone or trying to fix the water heater. They aren't always paying attention to their children. Even so, just being around a parent is an important part of growing up.

Bobbi was visiting her father for the summer when she had her first period. When she noticed that she was bleeding she knew what was happening to her body because her mother had talked to her about it beforehand. She wasn't scared, but she wanted to talk with her mom about this new development and there was the very practical consideration that her dad did not have any sanitary napkins or tampons in the house. She was embarrassed to ask him to run to the store and buy some, but she had no choice. When she asked him, she could feel that he was just as uncomfortable about what had happened as she was. He didn't know what to say to her. After he left, she decided to call her mom, and after they talked for a few minutes, Bobbi felt better.

Even when young adults have contact with both parents, instances like the one Bobbi experienced occasionally happen. Teenagers who rarely see a parent or whose parent has abandoned them have a bigger challenge than picking up the telephone. They often experience times when they want to talk, have to get some advice, or just need a shoulder to cry on, but no one is there for them except for their custodial parent, who can't fill that particular need.

Even though no one can be a perfect substitute for a parent, it is possible to find friendship, guidance, nurturing, and even some role modeling by interacting with other adults besides parents.

Because Bobbi and her mom both worked, they spent less and less time together. She found herself looking up to Mrs. Carver at the day care center and talking with her about her daily problems and the dreams she had in her life. She was glad that Mrs. Carver was there for her.

Organizations such as Big Brothers and Big Sisters arrange for adult volunteers to spend time with young adults who would benefit from the presence of another adult of the same sex in their lives. Teachers; coaches; and church, temple, or mosque youth leaders can also serve as sources for adult interaction. So can friends of the family.

In addition, aunts, uncles, and grandparents make good role models and adult friends for teenagers. When Jeremy's uncle flew in for a visit, they got to know each other pretty well. Jeremy liked the fact that he and his uncle shared the same sense of humor, and that his uncle liked sports just as much as he did. Even though his uncle had to leave after a week, the two became fast friends and promised to keep in contact. Jeremy made plans to visit him for a week during the summer. Even though getting to know his uncle better didn't make up for spending less time with his father, it did help.

Neighbors are often willing to pitch in for a parent who no longer fills that role full-time. Selena's best friend's father helped fix her 10-speed bike when it broke, and he even showed her how she could fix it the next time a similar problem developed. Sometimes he would take both girls swimming or jog with them in the park. Because he was willing to include her in his plans with his daughter, Selena found that even though she missed her father, she enjoyed getting to do the kinds of things she had done with him more frequently than she could during visits.

Building New Traditions

In addition to building independence and the self-esteem that comes with it, successfully meeting the challenges of divorce helps young adults and their families establish new traditions that can sometimes be more satisfying and enjoyable than the old ones.

The first Christmas after his mom and dad's divorce Jeremy spent the holiday with his father and alternated between feeling like he wanted to be in two places at once and feeling like he wanted to be nowhere at all. He was used to drinking the eggnog his father always prepared on Christmas Eve, and eating the Christmas cookies his mother made. He and his dad put up the tree and his sister and his mother trimmed it. They would get up early Christmas morning. After his mom put some carols on the stereo, they would all open presents. Even though his parents hadn't gotten along very well, Christmas had been different at his home, a time when everyone felt like a family.

By the second Christmas the family decided Jeremy and his sister would spend Christmas Eve at his dad's house and open presents, then he'd come back to his mom's on Christmas day before dinnertime. The holiday seemed a little bit odd at first, but having two Christmases and two Christmas dinners wasn't so terrible, especially when his friends said they envied him.

New family traditions don't center only around the holidays. After Bobbi's mom started working, she didn't always feel like cooking. Some evenings Bobbi prepared dinner and other times they all made their own sandwiches. Bobbi's mom cooked on the weekends, but she and her children established a habit of going out for pizza every Friday at an Italian restaurant down the street. It was a time for them to relax and forget their worries. They talked about what had gone on during the past week. At first, Bobbi missed not having her father there, but after a time, she was surprised because her mother and brothers felt like a family as they gathered around the table—a single-parent family—and she felt good being part of that circle.

Broken marriages don't necessarily leave broken young people in their wake. Most young adults whose parents divorce survive the stress and grief over the loss of a nuclear family. They discover that single-parent families can be positive places to grow up, and they move beyond day-to-day surviving to discovering strengths that they didn't know they had, and actually thriving. Although the lives of young people are changed by the fact that their parents couldn't live happily ever after together, change is an opportunity to grow. Life goes on. Teenagers whose parents divorce still have their future ahead of them. With the lessons they've learned from facing and overcoming the challenges of divorce, chances are it will be a good one.

7

Where to Find Help

Divorce Resources

Children's Rights Council
Suite 140
220 I (Eye) Street NE
Washington, DC 20002-4362
(202) 547-6227
http://www.vix.com/crc
An advocacy group, CRC works to assure a child frequent, meaningful, and continuing contact with two parents and extended family that he or she would normally have during a marriage. The group lobbies Congress and has a quarterly newsletter.

Divorce Online
http://divorce-online.com
Divorce Online is the largest divorce web site on the Internet today and provides an extensive list of links to other, more specialized pages that deal with legal and emotional divorce issues. The site features a list of articles about divorce, including several for teenagers.

National Congress for Men and Children
P.O. Box 171675
Kansas City, KS 66117
(800) 733-3237
NCMC provides information on custody and child support for single dads. They publish a newsletter and offer referrals.

National Organization of Single Mothers
P.O. Box 68
Midland, NC 28107
(704) 888-5437
A group which focuses on the needs of single-parent moms and their families. NOSM provides referrals and publishes a magazine.

One-Parent Families Association of Canada
6979 Yonge Street
Suite 203
Willowdale, Ontario
Canada   M2M 3X9
(416) 226-0062
This national organization provides learning resources and activities for single-parent families throughout Canada. Teens from single-parent homes can network with other teenagers like themselves.

Parents Without Partners International
401 North Michigan Avenue
Chicago, IL 60611
(312) 644-6610
http://www.parentswithoutpartners.org
This international organization offers referrals to local chapters that provide activities for single families and education for single parents. Some local chapters hold special meetings for teens.

Help for Specific Problems

Child Abuse/Domestic Violence

Kempe Children's Center
1825 Marion Street
Denver, CO 80218
(303) 864-5252
http://www.kempecenter.org
The Kempe Center is staffed by professionals who provide information and referrals. The organization actively works to stop child abuse.

National Clearinghouse on Childhood Abuse and Neglect
P.O. Box 1182
Washington, D.C. 20013
(800) 394-3366
This clearinghouse gathers and provides information on a variety of topics having to do with child abuse.

Women Helping Women
P.O. Box 552, Station U
Toronto, Ontario
Canada   M8Z 5T8
(416) 252-7949
This organization provides information and referrals about all kinds of violent crimes that happen to women and children, including domestic violence, rape, and child abuse.

Children of Chemically Dependent Parents

Adult Children of Alcoholics
6381 Hollywood Boulevard, Suite 685
Hollywood, CA 90028
(213) 464-4423
An organization based on the Twelve Steps program of Alcoholics Anonymous, ACA focuses on recovery for both young people and adults who were raised by an alcoholic parent.

Al-Anon/Alateen Family Group
(800) 356-9996
Alanon and Alateen members work on their own recovery from living with an alcoholic. The organization provides a free information packet, and can refer callers to local groups.

Al-Anon/Alateen Information Services
1712 Avenue Road
P.O. Box 54533
North York, Ontario
Canada   M5M 4N5
(416) 366-4072
This group provides the same information and services as the U.S. group.

Canadian Association for Children of Alcoholics
555 University Avenue
Box 200
Toronto, Ontario
Canada   M5G 1X8
(416) 813-5629
This group provides information and referrals for children of alcoholics throughout Canada.

Families Anonymous
(Families of Substance Abusers)
P.O. Box 528
Van Nuys, CA 91408
(818) 989-7841
Families Anonymous has more than 400 local chapters that help relatives and friends heal from the trauma that comes from loving someone who is chemically dependent.

Crisis and Suicide Hot Lines

Kids Help Phone
1 (800) 668-6868
http://kidshelp.sympatico.ca

A Canadian crisis line, Kids Help Phone offers crisis intervention in both English and French. The project also sponsors a web site covering family issues, eating disorders, drug abuse, child abuse, sexual violence, and suicide.

Youth Crisis Hotline
(800) HIT-HOME
Privately funded by Youth Development International, this crisis line specializes in intervention counseling and referrals for people 18 and under. They deal with any kind of crisis, including depression and suicide.

Eating Disorders

American Anorexia and Bulemia Association, Inc.
133 Cedar Lane
Teaneck, NJ 07666
(201) 836-1800
This self-help group provides information and referrals as well as guidelines on how to start a local group.

Anorexia Nervosa and Associated Disorders, Inc.
Box 5102
Eugene, OR 97405
(503) 686-7372
This group has over 200 local chapters, which are sponsored by professionals in the field of eating disorders. They can provide information and referrals to counselors.

Missing Children

Find the Children
11811 W. Olympic Boulevard
Los Angeles, CA 90064
(310) 477-6721
This national nonprofit group works to prevent parental kidnapping of children and helps to locate children. The services they provide are free of charge.

National Center for Missing and Exploited Children
2101 Wilson Blvd.
Suite 550
Arlington, VA 22201-3052
This organization gives legal and technical assistance in cases of child-snatching. They have local groups throughout the United States.

Missing Children's Registry
Royal Canadian Mounted Police
P.O. Box 8885
Ottawa, Ontario
Canada   K1G 3M8
This government agency helps locate missing children in Canada.

Stepfamilies

The Stepfamily Association of America
215 Centennial Mall South, Suite 212
Lincoln, NE 68508
1 (800) 735-0329
SAA publishes a newsletter and a book for stepfamilies. The group has more than 60 local chapters.

For Further Reading

Bolick, Nancy O. *How to Survive Your Parents' Divorce.* New York: Franklin Watts, 1994.

Booher, Dianna Daniels. *Coping . . . When Your Family Falls Apart.* New York: Julian Messner, 1988.

Glassman, Bruce. *Everything You Need to Know About Stepfamilies.* New York: Rosen Publishing Group, 1994.

Levine, Beth. *Divorce: Young People Caught in the Middle.* New York: Enslow Publishers, 1995.

Peters, Deanna, and Richard L. Strohm. *Divorce & Child Custody: Your Options and Legal Rights.* New York: Chelsea House Publishers, 1997.

Presma, Frances, and Paula Edelson. *Straight Talk About Today's Families.* New York: Facts On File, 1999.

Wagonseller, Bill R., Lynne C. Ruegamer, and Marie C. Harrington. *Coping in a Single-Parent Home.* New York: Rosen Publishing Group, 1995.

Index